Bill Sanders has a passion for teens. He i
with today's teens. Based on his first-hand experience talking with
thousands of teens and their parents each year, Bill shares specific
strategies and step-by-step suggestions for teaching your teens how to
live healthy, successful, godly lives.

JOSH MCDOWELL

Bill Sanders has written a helpful book for parents of teenagers. It is full
of real situation examples and useful suggestions. A solid parenting
resource.

JAY KESLER

Seize the Moment, Not Your Teen is a good book by a good guy. Beautiful
blend of the emotion of love and the practicality of logic, which
combined give beautiful insights—even wisdom—in dealing with our
kids during their most challenging years. Scripturally sound and
lovingly written.

ZIG ZIGLAR

As I have worked with Bill Sanders, I have always been impressed with
his insights into the needs of teens. His direct and constant contact with
them enables him to write to parents with honesty and accuracy. There
are many books on parenting, but Bill's book, *Seize the Moment, Not
Your Teen,* is more of a book on being a good parent—with the
emphasis on the parent, not the teen.

FLORENCE LITTAUER

In *Seize the Moment, Not Your Teen,* Bill Sanders has provided parents
with an outstanding resource. Drawing on his years of experience as
one of America's most gifted youth-communicators and as a father of
teenagers himself, Bill shares practical steps that parents can take to
nurture and teach their kids. I especially appreciate Bill's emphasis on
exercising positive disciplineandholding the line while doing everything
with love. He challenges parents to be positive role models, to stay
involved with their kids, and to take advantage of every God-given
opportunity to guide them in the right direction. Bill knows what he's
talking about, and he says it well!

DAVE VEERMAN

SEIZE
THE
MOMENT,
NOT YOUR TEEN

THE ART OF OPPORTUNITY PARENTING

BILL SANDERS

Tyndale House Publishers, Inc.

WHEATON, ILLINOIS

Visit Tyndale's exciting Web site at www.tyndale.com

Library of Congress Cataloging-in-Publication Data

Sanders, Bill, date
    Seize the moment, not your teen: the art of opportunity parenting / Bill Sanders.
      p. cm.
    ISBN 0-8423-6936-8 (softcover: alk. paper)
      1. Parenting—Religious aspects—Christianity.   2. Parent and teenager—Religious aspects—Christianity.   3. Parent and teenager.   4. Communicationin the family.   I. Title.
BV4529.S27   1997
248.8 45—dc21   96-48808

Printed in the United States of America

03 02 01 00 99 98
7   6   5   4   3

CONTENTS

Acknowledgments

God gets all the credit for any lives that are touched by this book. He told me to write it in the first place, and it has helped me be a much better parent and husband. God is awesome, and I've never been more committed to or in love with him.

My sisters, Mary and Jean, were used by the Lord to help determine the final direction of this book. I'm so glad they are in my life and that we are such close friends. I love you both very much. Thanks for living out your faith for all the world to see.

My longtime friend Mike McGeath has been a constant cheerleader and encourager in my speaking and writing. (I know he was just kidding when he said all of my books were the same material with different covers and titles!) Thanks for looking over parts of this and giving me ideas and editing tips.

Finally, I want to thank a great communicator named John Young. You have been so gracious over the past ten years, promoting my books through your radio programs in Atlanta. Every day for the last nine months of this project I read your words, "You've not written your best book yet. You're writing it right now!" Thanks for your prayers and belief in me.

Introduction

Parenting in the last half of the nineties can best be described by the opening line of *A Tale of Two Cities*: "It was the best of times, it was the worst of times." No society has ever been harder on families than ours, yet we live in a day when parents who pour love, time, and consistency into their kids' lives can see greater payoffs than ever before. Our children are starving for authenticity—seeing us live out our values and faith. When we do, they take notice because the world that surrounds them is overflowing with fakery, confusion, and selfish agendas.

I don't need to waste your precious time telling you how hard it is to stay married, raise kids, and keep your sanity. I have a hard enough time myself, keeping the spark alive between my wife and me and being an example for my own three kids to follow. What you and I both need to hear, however—and we need to hear it over and over again—is that God is pulling for us. His Holy Spirit dwells in us, able to keep us calm during frazzled times and full of wisdom when the rest of the world and half of the neighborhood are spinning out of control.

But here lies the problem: Most of us aren't Dr. James Dobson or Chuck Swindoll. We don't have the vision of Bill Hybels, the reputation of Billy Graham, or the expertise of the people at Minerth-Meier. And when I tell my kids about Jesus, it never comes out the way Max Lucado would say it. We aren't super-parents with all the answers. (Of course, neither are these men, and they would be the first to admit it.) Let's face the facts. Parenting as God would have us do it, in an age of garbage-filled talk shows and kids bringing guns to school each day, is over-whelming and an uphill battle at best.

Adding to our challenge is the fact that many of us are wounded in a world that makes us feel guilty if we are anything but strong and confident and have our kids starring in at least three different sports. Our inner voices call us hypocrites in so many different areas. We hear ourselves asking: How can I tell my kids not to use drugs if I did? What right do I have to lay a guilt trip on my child about premarital sex if I was weak in that area? And what about cheating, failing to show respect for parents, and living with so many unconfessed sins?

Every family has pain and troubles. No family has it all to-gether—not even the one who is always early to church and whose kids never act up in public. (Wouldn't you just love to hire a detective to follow them for a couple of weeks? Catch them on video! In the act! You know, things like not making their beds, leaving dirty dishes sitting around all day. And you've got to believe there is a room somewhere in that perfect-looking house that is piled three feet deep with bug-infested dirty clothes. Give me ten minutes in their house while they're gone and I'll get the goods on them!)

Jokes aside, I am fortunate to know several parents who do seem to have *most of it* together. They aren't perfect, but when they have to, they can tell their child, "I'm sorry" or "Please forgive me; I goofed up." They've developed the habit of forgiving their children when the children make them angry and of moving forward without dwelling on past mistakes. They live out their faith in public during the week as well as on Sunday mornings in church. They enjoy that peace that I've spent most of my adult life searching for.

I wrote this book for myself because I want to be more like those parents and even more like God. Come with me on the journey. Let's find out what God has to share about seizing the moment, not our teens.

CHAPTER 1

Making the Choice to Change

A NEIGHBOR and dear friend of mine stopped by our summer cottage one afternoon, and like a three-year-old with an exciting discovery, she shared, "Here's a cute story you can use in one of your speeches." She motioned for me to follow her to the picnic table. "As you know, my two grandkids are visiting. Grandpa and I took them to lunch and said, 'If you finish your entire meal, you can order any dessert you wish.' They love a challenge, so with one eye on us as we barely concealed our amazement at this rare feat—seldom attempted by other kids their age—they both devoured their meals. I looked at the twelve-year-old and asked what he wanted for dessert. He pointed to the largest dessert on the menu. It was one of those ice cream treats for a group of six. It cost over four dollars! He exclaimed, 'I want that one, Grandma!' I couldn't disappoint him, so I looked him in the eye and said, 'A deal's a deal!' Then the eight-year-old, who I'm sure will be president of something someday, closed the menu, looked at me with his wheels turning, and said, 'Grandma, if it's all the same to you, I'll take the cash!' Grandpa and I tried not to laugh out loud when the older one said with all the seriousness of a heart attack, 'But Grandma, I didn't *know* we had a *choice!*' "

Most people live the same way, not knowing they have a choice—a choice to change. If you are anything like me, you've probably had stretches in your life where you knew you needed to change in certain areas, but you thought things would run along smoothly—or maybe even get better—if you just did nothing at all.

In parenting, nothing could be further from the truth. Our children are constantly changing, and if we are to even keep up with them (let alone understand the latest phase they are going through) and parent effectively, change is a *must!*

Someone once told me, "If you always do what you've always done, you'll always get what you've always gotten." Think about it. If there is any area in your life that didn't go as well as you had hoped last year, it will most likely be just as bad this year unless some changes are made. And the choices and changes we make as parents have extremely high stakes: our children's lives.

TOMORROW NEVER COMES

"I'll do it tomorrow." "Not today!" "There is plenty of time." "I've earned the right to coast." We are all good at putting off what's best for us, whether it be healthier eating, exercising, or spending more time with God or our kids. Once and for all, let's get rid of the idea of making changes *tomorrow.*

Tomorrow never comes! To see for yourself, simply wait up until 11:59 p.m. and count the seconds. 11:59:57, 11:59:58, 11:59:59, 12:00! At the stroke of midnight, guess what you have? *Today!* Wait twenty-four more hours, and you will once again end up with *today.*

I ask thousands of teens each year if they are planning to stop drinking. They all say, "Tomorrow." When I ask about living for God, they say, "Tomorrow." It's the same with respecting their parents, making something of their lives, or stopping premarital sex. The answer is always "tomorrow."

Our prisons are filled with adults who are going to change "tomorrow." Alcoholics are everyday drinkers who kept drinking, and today is the tomorrow they enter with fear and uncertainty. Today's parents who live with low self-worth and feelings of inadequacy are yesterday's kids who weren't fortunate enough to have those healthy qualities instilled in them. The bottom line is this: Today's teens won't know how to be effective parents tomorrow if we don't decide to make needed changes today.

LIFE WITHOUT REGRETS IS WONDERFUL

My dad was dying of cancer. He had just a few months to live. He was having a good day with relatively little pain, and I asked him, "What do you wish you had done in your life that you never got the chance to do?" I thought he would say something about his lifelong desire to go to Hawaii (I can still hear him pronounce it "Hawieer"), or buy a brand, spanking, out-of-the-showroom new car. Without any thought or hesitation, he looked at me with pain and regret written all over his face and said, "That's not what I'm thinking about at all these days, Son. All I seem to be able to think about are all the things I *did* that I wish I had never done."

I'll never forget that statement. My greatest hero was challenging me to live without regrets. And I want to pass the challenge on to you. If there is someone you need to go to and ask forgiveness, please pray for the strength to do it. Free yourself from the pain that makes Satan so very happy. I think he delights as much in having God's children suffer because of sin and pride as he does in keeping unbelievers from God in the first place.

Is there bitterness in your heart over a past hurt or regret? Pray for strength to totally turn it over to God. He can handle it—you can't. His grace is sufficient. His love can cover a million regrets and sins. To have such a great and mighty God and not trust him totally to take care of our inner bleeding is as bad as not having him at all. To never turn the light switch on and live in total darkness makes the homeowner a fool. To push your car around town instead of driving it would be absurd. And yet that's what we do every time we continue to hang on to pain or choose not to change, all because deep down we don't think God is big enough to take care of it.

When we fail to turn to God in times of trouble we are like the psalmist who wrote, "Why am I discouraged? Why so sad? I will put my hope in God! I will praise him again—my Savior and my God!" (Psalm 43:5). However, when we put our faith into action we can pray, "You faithfully answer our prayers with awesome deeds, O God our savior. You are the hope of everyone on earth, even those who sail on distant seas" (Psalm 65:5).

I encourage you with all my heart to make the choice to change what must be changed and do what God is silently telling you to do, so you will never be consumed with regret on your deathbed as my dad was. Ahead of us are endless opportunities to grow.

OUR KIDS KNOW . . .

If you ever want to know what areas you need to change in, just ask your kids. What would they say if you asked them the following questions?

1. In what areas could I be more consistent?

2. To be a better parent, what should I stop doing?

3. What are some things I should do more of or start doing?

4. What changes could I make that would make it easier for you to come to me when you need to talk about something important?

5. What activities do you miss doing today that we did when you were younger?

GOD WOULD LOVE IT IF I . . .

Another way to decide what areas we need to change is to finish the sentence *God would love it if I* . . . Since we are looking for creative ways to teach our kids the lessons that will take them successfully into and through adulthood, we can seldom ask often enough what bad habits or traits they are picking up from us. When you start to do something you know is damaging to your family's best interest, think of what would make God the happiest. It's fun to find verses that will zap the desire to make Satan happy right out of you.

Whenever I find myself dwelling on someone who has hurt me, I try to remember Paul's words in Philippians 3:13-14: "I am focusing all my energies on this one thing: Forgetting the past and looking forward to what lies ahead, I strain to reach the end of the race and receive the prize for which God, through Christ

Jesus, is calling us up to heaven." Usually I remember Jesus saying that if I fail to forgive others, he won't forgive me. (Ooh, that one hurts. . . .)

When I want to be served and have the world revolve around me (I'm usually pretty happy when things go totally my way), I'm convicted by the love chapter—1 Corinthians 13: "Love is not . . . rude. Love does not demand its own way. Love is not irritable, and it keeps no record of when it has been wronged" (1 Corinthians 13:4-5). There is enough there to drive any parent or child to their knees in childlike humility, which is where God would like us to spend more of our time anyway.

Ask your kids to think over their last frustration or time of great worry. Ask what would have made God happy—the response they used or another? Take the opportunity to get to know your kids better and build the trust bond between you by discovering ways to please God by our responses to difficult times.

DON'T DO THE EASIEST THING
I learned this years ago! It's a wonderful way to test whether we are doing things God's way or living out the desires of our three worst enemies: the world, our fleshly desires, and the devil. Ask yourself, *Is this what Jesus would do, or am I just doing the easiest thing?* The easiest action in any given situation is usually the worst thing to do.

It's easier to sleep in instead of getting up a little early and starting our day with a special backstage pass to be one-on-one with the Creator of the universe. When our kids are in the middle of a shouting match, the easiest and most natural thing to do is join in and yell a little louder. Insert your thoughts with *volume*. We miss a key opportunity to reach our kids when we act out of habit instead of thinking things through.

Is it easier to give your hard-to-be-around fourteen-year-old toys and money instead of your time? One set of parents learned this lesson in a very bitter and tragic way. Their teen left this suicide note: "Dear Mom and Dad, you've given me everything to live life *with*. But nothing to live *for!*"

Make a list of your easiest and most-often-used reactions and replace them with godly responses. My list looked something like this:

Reactions that come easily	Godly responses
Yell at kids.	Talk calmly when angered.
Gossip about others.	Say only positive things about others.
Stay mad at people.	Forgive and forget.
Put children down.	Build them up with actions and words.
Tear spouse down in front of kids.	Support and forgive your mate. Pray for him or her.
Expect kids to be perfect.	Let kids be kids. Give them the freedom to grow up and goof up.
Get mad about poor grades.	Turn TV off and study with kids.
Eat when depressed.	Push yourself away from table and take a walk.
Become quiet when confronted.	Ask yourself if God is trying to tell you to change.

Tell kids you're too busy to spend time with them.	Say "thanks for asking."
Be too serious.	Find ways to fill your house with laughter.
Raise voice when kids make mistakes.	Encourage them to try new things.
Condemn your school.	Take an active role and get involved.
Let teens go to any party.	Talk with other parents to know what takes place.
Let TV become a baby-sitter.	Give ten tokens a week— one for each TV hour.
Give up on strong-willed child.	Never give up. God changes people.

As you make your list, try to identify the typical situations that frustrate you the most. Don't fall for the same temptations year after year. Stay strong, and rely on Jesus' strength to respond in a godly way instead of reacting habitually because it takes less thought and effort.

GET A PLAN

Whatever the areas you need to make changes in, get a plan and get going.

First, write down exactly what you want to do and when you intend to do it. You must be specific: *Lose fifteen pounds within three months. Read one book a week. Pray with each child every night. Learn to play the piano by such-and-such a date.*

Next, determine at least two steps that will help ensure that you will reach your goal. For instance, to lose fifteen pounds your two steps might be to see a doctor for a complete physical and to eat only a certain number of calories each day. In order to read a book in a week you might need to turn off the TV from eight to nine each night and read forty pages. You'll have read a two-hundred-page book in five nights. In order to pray with each child every night, you will need to be organized and ready for the challenge. If you have three kids with the same bedtimes, you may need to stagger the prayer times so that each one gets one-on-one time with you. Or you may need to pray together, giving special time to a different child each night. The main thing is to break your goal down into two or more bite-size pieces.

Third, tell someone else about your goal and the steps you want to take. It's vital that a trusted friend knows about your goal and is as committed to your success as you are. Give this person a written record of your goal. Sign it. Have your friend call you periodically to check up on you. (Incidentally, this can be a great reciprocal arrangement—you can do the same thing for your friend.)

Finally, pray for strength every day. Remember, we can do all things with God's strength. Don't try to make great things happen, in your own life or your family's, without the help of God.

ENDLESS OPPORTUNITIES TO GROW

In each chapter of this book, we will discover practical ways to help our kids, especially our teens. If we put these suggestions all together, by the end of the book we will have had endless opportunities to grow. If some of the suggestions aren't for you, don't worry about them. Merely move on to one that is and put it into practice. A big part of "opportunity parenting" (making the most of every situation that arises throughout the day) is staying consistent and strong. These practical challenges will help us stay in shape, so to speak, so when teachable moments arrive, we can teach what God wants us to instill in our children.

Before my grandmother's death at the age of ninety-seven, she had asked that her Bible be given to me as a special remembrance of her. Inside the front cover I found this poem, which my grandmother tried very hard to live by. This poet's prayer is my prayer. I hope it inspires you to change in your needed areas as it has me.

Christ—My Children—My Death

When I am dead and gone to rest,
The minister will do his best
To say kind things, and try to prove,
That I have lived, just as I should.
But what will my dear children say,
When my casket is shut that day?

My children know my petty faults,
My selfishness and vanity;
My love for righteousness and truth,
And justice and sincerity.
Then just what will their verdict be,
When saying their farewell to me?

O Lord, my Lord, I pray, I pray,
Direct my faltering steps each day;

Strengthen my hands and knees each hour,
In life bestow the Spirit's power,
In death, cause my children to see
My Christ in all his deity.

WHAT ABOUT YOU?

1. If you were to die today, what would you want to be remembered for?

2. If you knew you would never see your family again, what regrets would you have?

3. What habits have you always wanted to develop? Why not come up with a written plan and a committed friend to help you be accountable? Put the needed prayer and effort into it and make yourself proud.

4. What skills do you wish your children had that they don't have at this time? Make a list. Ask yourself if they are gaining these skills by watching you day by day. (I know, this one hurts me, too, when I put it to the test with my kids.) What changes could you choose to make so your kids would have a more positive role model to follow?

5. What could you do daily to make God happy? Since tomorrow never comes, why not please him today by putting this thought into action?

6. What's one thing you could do each week or month to show the love of Jesus to someone else? Your kids or your Bible study group could brainstorm ideas with you.

7. How would you feel if someone else treated your child the way you do? When a friend asked me this question, I saw several shortcomings in myself that I had never seen before.

EXTRA POWER FOR PARENTS FROM GOD'S WORD

> Remain in me, and I will remain in you. For a branch cannot produce fruit if it is severed from the vine, and you cannot be fruitful apart from me. Yes, I am the vine; you are the branches. Those who remain in me, and I in them, will produce much fruit. For apart from me you can do nothing. (John 15:4-5)

"Remaining in" Jesus means staying close to him, gaining strength from the Bible, and talking to him daily. Our goal as parents is to bear the right kind of fruit. Our children are the fruit of our labors, the reason God put us in this job in the first place. Never try to raise kids (or achieve anything worthwhile) all by yourself without God's power and Holy Spirit working in you. Raise your kids on the right vine.

> Those who become Christians become new persons. They are not the same anymore, for the old life is gone. A new life has begun! (2 Corinthians 5:17)

When you trust Jesus Christ for your salvation, you become a new person. You can move away from the old you that didn't care if you pleased or hurt God by your lifestyle. Refuse to remain the old you. Change. Grab ahold of the Lord's hand, and get to know him like never before. Change and grow and never again accept anything less than God's very best for you or your family.

> And the one who sent me is with me—he has not deserted me. For I always do those things that are pleasing to him. (John 8:29)

Jesus is our constant example, and he is worth following. God wants to stay with us constantly as well. Pleasing him puts us in a special place in God's eye. The benefits are fantastic as well.

> When the ways of people please the Lord, he makes even their enemies live at peace with them. (Proverbs 16:7)

Just think—if pleasing God makes our enemies get along with us, our family life is headed for some great times! List the ways your family can do things that are pleasing to the Lord. Look at specific areas such as getting along with each other around the house, your teen's choice of friends, your family devotion time, your family's testimony to the neighbors, and the way you negotiate solutions with your spouse or children.

CHAPTER 2

Daily Vitamins for Parents of All Ages

DURING ONE of my parent seminars, an interesting discussion took place between me and a wise old farmer. Five hundred other community members listened in and enjoyed it immensely.

I was using the legs of a chair to illustrate the four areas of strength each of us needs in order to be well balanced. I was referring to Luke 2:52, which describes Jesus during those blackout years of his teens and twenties. The Bible tells us nothing about this period of his life except to say that he grew in four main areas: physical, mental, spiritual, and social. "Jesus grew both in height [physical] and in wisdom [mental], and he was loved by God [spiritual] and by all who knew him [social]."

I held up a chair to show that four legs were sturdier than three or two. Someone yelled, "What about a farmer's milking stool? They seem very sturdy, yet they have only *one* leg."

In the middle of the crowd a hand arose and calmly waved to get my attention.

"Yes, sir," I said, hoping he could help me out. "Do you have any insights on farmers' stools?"

He replied in a down-to-earth manner, "I should have a little. I've used one for the past thirty years. It's true that there is only one leg on the stool. However, the second and third *foundational* legs are the two feet of the person milking, which I might add are usually mine."

All eyes in the school auditorium were on him.

He continued, "The fourth leg of any milker worth his salt is his shoulder. It's buried in the side of old Bessie. Just like you said, I need all four legs, or I'll fall flat on my face."

In this chapter we'll take a look at how we can use all four legs to stay balanced and strong as parents. We will look at each of the four areas that Jesus developed in as he grew into adulthood. If we want our children to be "difference makers," we must model these four areas of *foundational stability.*

THAT'S MY BOD!

The first area Jesus grew in was height—physical growth. Growing up as the son of a carpenter, he was hardworking and active. And having no car, he stayed in good physical shape by walking. But in our modern society, how can *we* take the weight off and stay in shape—even Oprah with all her resources can't do it! Face it; in America today, with tasty temptations everywhere, it's extremely difficult to eat properly and stay in shape . However, I firmly believe that if we aren't able to keep up with our kids physically, we will be hurting our chances to be the most effective role models possible.

It doesn't matter what athletic ability you have; there are perfect exercises for each of us. If jogging is not your thing, try walking. If basketball is too strenuous, play tennis. Invest in a complete physical exam to see what shape you truly are in and what diet and exercise program fits you.

Have you ever looked into the refrigerator and nothing looked good? That means you aren't hungry. Here's a little trick you can use: Step 1, shut the door. Step 2, take your hand off the handle. Step 3, leave the kitchen! Exercise gurus never told you that, but it works.

It would be unthinkable to own a fifty-thousand-dollar car and never change the oil or refuse to give it tune-ups at the recommended times. Yet we treat our bodies as if they were old junkers. We forget that the wheels we were given at birth must last us all the way through this trip of a lifetime. God wants us to take care of his temple. We need to be on twenty-four-hour-a-day watch to know exactly what goes into this remarkable creation, as well as discerning carefully what we demand from it.

If I'm not paying special attention to my physical needs, such as getting enough sleep, eating enough fruits and vegetables, exercising a little each day, and being very careful about what I eat late at night, I say and do things that I almost always regret. Get to know yourself. When you feel good physically, it's much easier to stay strong in the other areas as well. Pray for wisdom and strength in taking care of yourself. Many people spend their whole lives looking forward to retirement, only to realize when they get there that they are too tired or sick to enjoy it. Life is to be lived out and enjoyed each day as it comes, not dreaming about days and times that may never arrive.

THINK ABOUT IT

Every living thing has two options. It either grows or dies. It doesn't matter if it is a flower or a parent. Coasting simply doesn't work for very long, because it's always downhill. As parents trying to keep a step ahead of our kids and their culture, we must stay sharp mentally. It would benefit each of us as parents to be on constant lookout for ways to keep our mental muscles in top shape.

I've been discussing and studying Luke 2:52 for many years. I've often wondered why *wisdom* came before *spiritual* development. The Bible answered it for me: It tells me that true wisdom can only come from God. My synonym finder says *wisdom* means "perception, discernment, understanding, sound judgment, clear thinking, foresight," and—my favorite—"mother wit." All the parents I've ever met who have teens that respect them have these qualities. Those parents read more than they watch TV, and they know at almost all times where their teens are. They live out and teach the skill of discernment. Wise parents understand the need for clearly defined boundaries and rules.

When it's time for your teen to do homework, turn off the TV and grow mentally yourself by reading something that interests you or causes you to stretch and grow. With fewer than 5 percent of Americans reading even one book each year, it takes very little effort to move from the ranks of the status quo. Our minds, just like our muscles, get flabby and atrophied if they aren't challenged on a consistent basis.

Our children's desire for reading, using the computer, daring to learn new ways of doing old things, will not be *taught* by our words but needs to be *caught* by their seeing our own continual growth in this area. Our kids strive to be like us, even to the extent of growing and changing—or refusing to do so.

The book of James points out two kinds of wisdom—godly and worldly.

If you are wise and understand God's ways, live a life of steady goodness so that only good deeds will pour forth. And if you don't brag about the good you do, then you will be truly wise! But if you are bitterly jealous and there is selfish ambition in your hearts, don't brag about being wise. That is the worst kind of lie. For jealousy and selfishness are not God's kind of wisdom. Such things are earthly, unspiritual, and motivated by the Devil. For wherever there is jealousy and selfish ambition, there you will find disorder and every kind of evil.

But the wisdom that comes from heaven is first of all pure. It is also peace loving, gentle at all times, and willing to yield to others. It is full of mercy and good deeds. It shows no partiality and is always sincere. And those who are peacemakers will plant seeds of peace and reap a harvest of goodness. (James 3:13-18)

What a beautiful description of children growing in the grace and favor of God—"a harvest of goodness."

Look each day for creative ways to keep your mental strength growing. And remember: "If you need wisdom—if you want to know what God wants you to do—ask him, and he will gladly tell you. He will not resent your asking." (James 1:5)

DON'T JUST SIT IN THE PEW!

Growing spiritually means taking your faith to new heights daily. Never settle for anything less than God's very best in your life. Many people sit in the same pew week after week, Sunday after Sunday, expecting to be entertained and reached and challenged without putting forth any effort themselves. Each of us would be wise to realize that God is not on stage Sunday morning—we are. He is watching us, waiting for us to glorify him by our worship and sincerity.

As Christians we can either live out the abundant life or be as miserable as those around us who haven't even had a glimpse of God's saving grace and love. Each and every morning, ask God to cleanse you from your sins and fill you with his Holy Spirit. Bill Bright, founder of Campus Crusade for Christ, told me that every morning he prays that he won't lose his first love—Jesus. If he has to go through the basics every morning, then I guess it's OK for the rest of us as well.

Spend whatever time you need to get God's attention and receive his blessing. I'm not implying that he isn't listening, but for *your* sake, don't try to get in touch with the God of gods and Lord of lords with a quick, flippant, microwave prayer on your way out the door with a thousand other things on your mind.

Learn a lesson from your children. When they want something from you, they don't stop bugging you until they receive it. God honors persistence. If our heart is pure and we ask to see and hear from our Creator, he will show himself.

The life-filled, abundant way of living is waiting for each of us. I believe we live in a very special time in which God has extra amounts of grace and joy to spill out upon his children. But to be a child who is too busy to spend time with his Father, too ashamed to be known as part of that family, or too prideful and rebellious to be obedient, is to be a child who is actually running away from the warmth and wealth of his family. Our cities are filled with far too many runaways. Their parents cry out for a phone call every night. Our heavenly Father cries out for our childlike return as well. If you have been the prodigal son or daughter, run back to your Daddy's waiting, outstretched arms.

Realizing that God knows more than we do, it would be wise to listen more than we speak. I find that all too often I treat God like a perpetual Santa Claus, only coming to him when I need things. He wants to be our very best friend and closest companion. He will never leave a child out in the cold alone. By living close to the Lord and talking to him on a regular basis, discerning what to do and how to live moment by moment, we will be able to enjoy God's very best as well as pass on an invaluable legacy to our kids.

Bill Hybels taught me several years ago how to have a rewarding experience in my morning quiet time with God and at the same time not fall asleep. When we've gotten up in the early hours to grab a glimpse of God, it's easy to be so tired that our prayers don't make sense or we lose interest before we have gained a proper audience with the king. This technique is not only simple but acts like free counseling. Simply write out your prayers to God as if they were a love letter addressed to him, following this outline:

Start with praise.

Start by giving God praise. Quite often I read the Psalms and write them down or put them in my own words. Can you imagine how special you would feel if your kids told you every morning how wonderful you were and how much they loved you for your special qualities? Your desire the rest of the day would be to do special things for them and honor them with blessing upon blessing. It's the same between God and us.

Confess your sins.

The second step in writing out your prayer is to admit your mistakes. Write out your sins and ask God for his wonderful forgiveness. This is where this journaling technique can act as free counseling. After a few days of confessing the same mistake, you feel ashamed to go before your Savior without turning from that sin. It feels so refreshing to be able to talk to God himself with no interruptions and receive a full measure of his attention and love and grace, day after day. Counseling costs ninety dollars an hour for the same undivided attention with only a drop of the wisdom and strength God can offer—free of charge.

Tell God what you need.

Now comes the easy part! Ask, ask, ask, and you will receive, receive, receive. The main requirement is that you desire the answer *he* feels is best for you—even more than you desire the answer *you* want. After we walk with God long enough, we'll want only what he wants for us.

Many people think they should approach God only with life-threatening issues. Nothing could be further from the truth. God is as interested in your vague and small problems as you are in those of your own children. If he has taken the time to number your hairs, he cares enough to give you strength all day long to handle each part of life and defeat every one of Satan's darts thrown at your weak areas.

Talk to God as you would to anyone you totally trust. Many people find it extremely difficult to talk to God or write him a letter on an intimate level because they've never had this wonderful form of dialogue modeled for them. You may want to discuss this with someone who has a close walk with God, or merely pray for help and start trusting and writing.

Thank God for everything.
The fourth step is almost miraculous in the way it eliminates worry and stress: Be thankful. Count your blessings one by one. Write them down. Be specific. A long list filled with seemingly little blessings is much more powerful than a short list of earth-shattering things. For instance, instead of writing down the word *family,* put the names of each child, your spouse, your parents, your grandparents, and so on. Mention many physical blessings, such as eyes, ears, healthy heart, ability to walk, think, speak, and laugh, instead of just writing the word *health.* List your special friends one by one. Name as many specific blessings as you can think of each morning. With prayer and awareness, you will find that your number of blessings can grow day by day as you think of new ones that you have probably taken for granted until now.

REAL LIVE ADULTS!
Growing socially. It has a nice ring to it, don't you think? But making our social lives a priority takes lots of effort. In the next two chapters, we'll be looking at ways our actions speak louder to our kids than our words do. And we'll see that spending time with our kids is essential to building a strong relationship with them. Very few parents can be accused of spending too much time communicating with their teens. However, once again we find that balance is the key. Parents can easily go to the extreme of becoming totally wrapped up in their kids' lives. They may sacrifice so much of their own lives that they become a "human doing" instead of a "human being."

It's extremely easy for socializing and having a date night with your spouse to become low priorities for months or years at a time. The world we live in does not encourage couples to fall back in love with each other on a regular, ongoing basis. Growing in this fourth area is just as tough as the other areas we've looked at.

In order to grow socially, you must be around people—living, breathing *people*. The best part is that they need to be your age. Make time to get out of the house without the kids and participate in a couples' Bible study, join a bowling, tennis, or golf league, or enjoy a favorite hobby with others you enjoy being around.

Some "social" time should also be spent apart from your spouse, so you can do your thing and experience life as an individual. I play golf with a group of guys each summer. Holly has friends she enjoys playing tennis with. Couples who feel like they can't let each other out of their sight aren't as socially healthy as they could be. They remind me of a T-shirt that says, "Togetherness—Ugh!" (Don't get mad! I'm merely suggesting that it's OK to enjoy a social outing now and then without your spouse.) The main thing is to grow and try new activities. You can do it. Your entire life will be blessed when you are around others on a regular basis doing something you enjoy.

WHAT ABOUT YOU?

1. What love and nurturing did you miss out on in your childhood? How can you seek it out today? It's very healthy to make a list of the mental, physical, spiritual, and social vitamins we never received as children. Write down the different types of hugs the child in you is still longing for. A wonderful book that fills me with all

types of emotional hugs as well as spiritual truth is *His Thoughts Toward Me* by Marie Chapian (Bethany House, 1987). It seems as though this book speaks to the little five-year-old Billy Sanders inside me. It's refreshing and wonderful every day to read these short devotions as if Jesus were talking directly to me.

2. At the end of a long, hard day, what do you wish you had done for yourself but didn't or couldn't? Think of how you could take some time out from your day tomorrow to do something special for yourself. Why not try it today? When I am home during the day, my wife, Holly, and I love to sit down to an inexpensive but wonderful afternoon treat—Café Vienna, delicious-tasting flavored coffee. It seems like a simple thing, but we try to carve out the last forty minutes before the kids come home from school to relax together. My office is in the house, so we shut down everything in order to treat ourselves and make some sense out of our typically hectic days. When Jesus was tired he got away from the crowds and treated himself to some peace and quiet.

3. If you were to die today, would the many activities that drain your energy still get done? Ask yourself if your laundry or yard work own you. Many people think they own their house, but in reality their house owns them. It's OK to realize that we are not indispensable. Everything will get done in due time, so don't let your busy schedule and this crazy-paced world keep you from taking care of yourself. Dip your finger into a bucket of water, pull it out, and watch how quickly the ripples disappear. You won't be forgotten quite that quickly, but the need for you to be so involved with energy-eating activities while not taking care of yourself should be brought into full focus.

4. Are there ways in which you can train your team (have you ever noticed how seldom we look at our family as our supporting team?) to help out with household chores or other responsibilities that bury you? Why not call a family meeting and ask each member what perks they would like that they feel cheated out of? Help each other free up time to give each family member their needed vitamins.

5. Do you feel guilty when you think about taking time for yourself? Why do you think you feel this way? How can you reprogram yourself to truly believe you are a miracle from God who needs attention in order to raise healthy, capable children? Write down a plan. Who can help you? Get going. You will never be all you can be for your children or God if you don't get over feeling guilty about being nice to yourself.

6. Do you feel you always have to fix the world? I have lived most of my adult life trying to be the peacekeeper and feeling guilty if I failed to fix something. If you have ever fallen into this trap, you know how futile it can be. It is absolutely wonderful turning things over to God instead of trying to carry them on my own weak shoulders. Give God what only he can handle—other people and their problems. Give your weak areas over to Jesus as well. You'll feel like dancing.

7. Have you been taught that the meaning of *JOY* is Jesus first, Others second, Yourself last? There is a great deal of truth in this formula but also a lot of confusion. For the person who is healthy emotionally and has a positive self-image, this three-step process works very well. On the other hand, trying to live by this formula can make a person who was put down, abused, or abandoned as

a child bitter toward those who are getting more attention—namely, Jesus and others. And life can be pretty rough when you are mad at God and others. I am not saying to put Jesus in any position other than first place, but I am encouraging you, if this applies, to start seeing yourself as God sees you.

I'm talking about a healthy biblical view of oneself. We are told to love our neighbors as ourselves. How can we give away what we don't possess? It's impossible. Let God show you how to think good thoughts about yourself. He made you the way you are, and loves you so much that he sent his only Son to give up his very life for you.

EXTRA POWER FOR PARENTS FROM GOD'S WORD

Jesus grew both in height and in wisdom, and he was loved by God and by all who knew him. (Luke 2:52)

The word I want each of us to focus on is *grew*. Are you growing, and if so, what are you doing to make sure you don't fall back to where you were in the past? What are you doing on a regular basis to ensure that you move ahead in the mental, physical, spiritual, and social areas? Challenge a friend or your Sunday school group to develop personal plans that will ensure moving ahead in each of these four areas just as Jesus did.

And so, dear Christian friends, I plead with you to give your bodies [physical] to God. Let them be a living and holy sacrifice—the kind he will accept [spiritual]. When

> you think of what he has done for you, is this too much to ask? Don't copy the behavior and customs of this world [social], but let God transform you into a new person by changing the way you think [mental]. Then you will know what God wants you to do, and you will know how good and pleasing and perfect his will really is. (Romans 12:1-2)

These verses cover the same four areas as Luke 2:52. We are each challenged to grow as Jesus did. Our bodies are to be as living sacrifices. Many say they would die for Jesus—but what about living for him in such a way that our very bodies are a testimony? We've been instructed to live in a holy and pure way for the Lord. He says this will please him. "Don't copy the behavior and customs of this world" is our next command. We are finally told how this all can take place: by letting God change the way we think. We make our minds new and full of wisdom by immersing them in God's life-giving Word on a regular basis.

> Don't worry about anything; instead, pray about everything. Tell God what you need, and thank him for all he has done. If you do this, you will experience God's peace, which is far more wonderful than the human mind can understand. His peace will guard your hearts and minds as you live in Christ Jesus. (Philippians 4:6-7)

This passage gives the greatest set of vitamins I've ever seen to ensure that stress and worry won't knock at your door. As you look carefully at—and I hope memorize—these verses, try to discover the steps to avoiding stress and worry.

First, we are *commanded not to worry*. God does not want

us to tolerate anxiety or worry, for it will damage our fellow-ship with the Holy Spirit. It's as if we are saying to God, "I cannot trust you with my troubles because you aren't capable of handling them." God alone can help us with so many difficult worries and struggles, but our pride and stubborn nature make us think we are smarter than the God who created us.

We are then asked to *pray about everything,* all the while *being thankful* for all of God's many blessings bestowed upon us. As we learned earlier in this chapter, it's nearly impossible to be depressed while looking at a long list of blessings and evidences of God's grace in our lives.

If we would only trust God and his words in this passage, we would have such joy that all the words in the dictionary could not fully describe it. Give your cares to the Lord and bathe in the beauty of his love.

> "For I know the plans I have for you," says the Lord. "They are plans for good and not for disaster, to give you a future and a hope." (Jeremiah 29:11)

Your loving Father wants to cuddle you in his love. All of his plans for you are good. Don't let the lies of this age or your past keep you prisoner for even another second. You have believed that you aren't worthy of God's greatest blessings and joys. But you are! Your negative, damning thoughts about yourself have pinned you to the mat of hopelessness. God, our loving Daddy, wants to replace our scars with laughter and our wounds with hugs and healing. Please allow him to love you, and then let it bubble out of you for all the world to see.

CHAPTER 3

Kids Hear Best with Their Eyes

IT WAS the chance of a lifetime. Along with two hundred other youth speakers, I had been invited by Josh McDowell himself. We had met only once before, but we had hit it off like two old friends bumping into each other after a long absence. During the entire flight from Michigan to California I was full of excitement and anticipation. Josh was kicking off his Why Wait? campaign, and I was invited to the party.

Arriving at the airport, I was met by a very professional-looking Campus Crusade staff member holding a sign that said "Bill Sanders." I felt like a visiting dignitary! A pleasant talk with lots of questions on my part got me all the way to the Campus Crusade headquarters. As I entered the registration area, which was filled with many conversations and even more food, I spotted Josh busily getting someone registered. As I watched, he grabbed the registrant's bags and motioned for him to follow him up the steps, two at a time, to his assigned room. A few moments later, Josh returned with seemingly endless energy and a servant's heart to personally take care of his next invited guest. I found out later that he had carried bags for his guests for nearly twenty hours with very few rests in between.

I've studied and watched people for years, but I had never

seen anything quite like this. The first chance I got, I pulled Josh aside and asked him why he did it. His answer will stay etched on my mind forever, an ongoing reminder to serve my wife and children with the same energy Josh used to wait on us. He put his hand on my shoulder and said simply, "My hero washed feet."

What amazed me most over the next several days was the cooperative atmosphere during all of Josh's seminar sessions. Not once did he have to speak on being a servant or a worthy leader. We had all seen it in action the very first day as he let his bag-handling skills do his speaking for him.

In this chapter I hope to help you become more aware of the many ways in which our actions shout. I also want to challenge you to become very serious about making your deeds match what comes from your mouth. St. Francis of Assisi's words would be a great statement for every parent to memorize and live out: "We are instructed to take the gospel into all the world and if we must, use words."

The old saying "actions speak louder than words" can be rephrased to help us keep our eyes peeled for opportunities to teach valuable lessons to our teens: "Kids hear best with their eyes!"

WORDS WHISPER; ACTIONS SHOUT

As we look at a number of everyday statements followed by actions that either back up those words or tear them down, you will understand the importance of staying strong and balanced in all areas of our lives, as we discussed in the last chapter. This is no job for the weak of heart. In fact, you may want to pour yourself a hot cup of tea and get relaxed before we start looking through a microscope at some very common diseases that we believers in Jesus have contracted from the world. Most of these aren't terminal, but all of them are very nauseating to God. Things like little white lies, exaggerations, gossip, unkept promises, hypocritical statements, and asking questions even when we aren't interested in the answers. Hang on to your tea—here we go.

Hi, how are you?

Let's start with an easy one. While walking into church, you say to a friend whom you haven't seen in a while, "Hi, how are you?" You continue walking, however, not noticing the slumped-over shoulders and listless eyes. Your friend pauses, raises his index finger, and starts to share—but you are too busy whisking past, wondering if anyone will notice your new outfit. Someone else noticed the entire event, however, as he was walking by your side—your fourteen-year-old son.

We've all been guilty of the above scenario, and what's even worse is that it often happens in our own home. Little by little our words lose their meaning, and teenagers find it easy to laugh off rules and instructions they don't feel like obeying. I've asked thousands of junior high and high school kids why they write me letters asking for advice instead of going to their parents. The answer I receive more than any other is this: "My parents don't really care how I am doing. They may ask me to share, but they only want to hear good news. When I tell them the truth, they either don't believe it or go ballistic." As God's stewards over our children, we need to say what we mean and mean what we say.

You might be thinking, *If that was the easy one, I'm not sure I wish to hear any more illustrations.* The problem is that there are many more, and since my kids remind me of them all the time, I thought I would spread the misery around and share some more with you.

I love you.

The words *I love you* are like a spring rain on the desert to our kids. That is, of course, as long as one sibling is not favored over another. I remember counseling a very despondent teen who was thinking about suicide. She reminded me of the Smothers brothers when they would always say, "Mom liked you best." This girl who thought she had nothing to live for kept telling me she knew in her heart that her parents favored her older sister. It had left her with little hope, since the two people that she needed most to believe in her didn't.

It doesn't really matter if the parents did or didn't favor the older sister. Perception is truth in the eyes of the beholder. This girl *thought* she was second best, and until she is convinced otherwise, nothing will change her mind. Let's face it; some kids are easier to love and get along with than others— especially if a son or daughter has the same personality you do. Having to go to God for help in loving your family members is nothing to be ashamed of. Most parents have dry spells from time to time when they have to sort out life issues for themselves, leaving very little energy and emotion for their children. But children, especially confused teens, often interpret times like these as no one loving them. Remember, when your children perceive that you like work or a hobby more than you like them, do whatever you have to to convince them otherwise.

Do as I say, not as I do.

It's hard for me to believe how much money teens have to spend on such things as movies and music these days. What is even more disturbing is the type of damaging material flooding into their impressionable minds. When I ask teens why they watch what they do, eight out of ten times they tell me their parents watch the same stuff. Because of this, my wife and I have decided not to watch R-rated movies to set an example for our own kids. Many parents tell me they watch the movies of their choice after the younger kids are in bed. They don't give their kids the credit they deserve. After kids reach the age of eight, they pretty much know most of our good and bad habits. If you decide not to change, don't be surprised in a few years if they are doing exactly what you have tried to hide.

Another painful example: I had to get rid of my fuzz buster. Kids call things as they see them. Fuzz busters are used to avoid the police and get away with speeding. If I want my kids to respect and obey the law, I need to do so—consistently—myself. (I told you these were going to be hard!)

Sure, you're important to me.

Dear Bill,

My dad is always telling me how important I am to him. Funny thing, he never has time for me and would rather be doing anything rather than spending time with me. When I do get a chance to be with him, he can't look me in the eye and is almost afraid to hug me. You can go ahead and tell me I'm special and God loves me and all that other good stuff, but none of that matters because my dad doesn't want to be around me.

The girl who wrote that letter symbolizes thousands of young people all across our country, and sadly enough many of them live in Christian homes. If our teens are going to make their mark on this world in a positive way, they must feel confident that they mean everything to us.

I have seen many surveys on successful teens vs. at-risk kids, and the results are always the same. One survey showed that the majority of men and women in prisons were told repeatedly by an authority figure in their life, "Someday you are going to go to jail." Another survey concluded that in order for a person to grow into a successful, confident, capable adult, there must be someone who is crazy about that person at every stage of his or her life.

wow!

We parents often forget that fulfilling our prophecies is the ongoing, never-ending task of our kids. What we say to them and about them they take as gospel truth.

Think about it. You like yourself best when someone is making a big deal over your big and small accomplishments. The memory of having my entire family watch my Little League ball games, cheering for me wildly in the bleachers, still gives me warm feelings and confidence today. Let's never give our kids a reason to wonder how important they are to us.

Of course I love Jesus.

A father recently told me that he felt his faith was continually letting him down and not supplying him with the strength he needed to raise his kids. After we talked for a short time, the answer

OR SHE

stared both of us in the face. He wasn't putting anything into his walk with the Lord—so why should he be receiving any benefits? He seldom read his Bible and felt uncomfortable praying, either alone or at church. He expected one hour in church on Sunday morning to carry him through the week. That's as crazy as eating breakfast on Monday and expecting to feel full on Saturday.

I am proud to tell you that I am so very weak that if I miss my morning time alone with God, I haven't the strength or composure to pass on the love God has for my kids. Refer back to chapter 2 from time to time to be reminded of the daily vitamins we must take to properly handle the toughest job ever handed down to mankind—parenting.

A good sign of being in love with someone is a magnetlike tug that makes you spend lots of time with that person. Think of the time when you first fell in love. You thought about and talked about that person with endless energy. You wrote poems and letters until your hand ached. Your constant question was, "Has he/she called yet today?" When you anticipated being with the one you loved, you took three times as long as normal brushing your teeth and combing your hair, you used twice as much deodorant, and while we could go on and on, you basically made a fool of yourself and didn't care. Our love for the Lord should be *ten times* as strong with *ten times* more evidence to anyone watching us. Until we become serious about our walk with the Lord, we will never be able to attract our kids to the trust, forgiveness, and grace of God.   *OUCH!*

God can do anything.

Have you ever had an almost impossible time turning something totally over to God? Have there been times in your life when worry and fear seemed to engulf you? Your answer is probably like that of every other Christian who has ever lived—a resounding *yes!*

If we get right down to it, the truth of the matter is that most of the time *we don't trust God.* It's natural to feel capable of getting yourself out of the dilemmas you find yourself in. After all, we get ourselves into messes in the first place, so it only makes sense that we should be able to get ourselves out of them. But we keep forgetting one thing: Only God can do certain things. We are the piece of clay. He is the master clay molder.

When we tell our kids that God is all-powerful and can help them with any problem they will ever encounter but then continue to worry about our own troubles, we confuse our kids. And worse, we become hypocrites. What's even more tragic is that God never has a chance to prove himself to us, and our kids don't get a chance to see faith in action being modeled.

Praying with your teens is one of the most wonderful ways for you to get to know and appreciate each other. They will see you differently than they have ever seen you before. Prayer also proves that you believe in a listening and capable God, one who can and will honor the words of an upright and godly person. As a family dedicated to God, you can hold each other up in daily prayer, so you will have the strength to turn from each temptation the devil throws your way.

God can do everything and anything—even take care of you. Please let him wrap his loving arms around you and help you with every pain you face. Why not spend a moment right now telling him how much you love and need him? Commit from this moment on to turn every trial over to God. Like a father waiting for his strong-willed child to run back to his arms asking for forgiveness and saying, "I love you, Daddy," the Lord is bubbling with excitement to hold you closely once again.

DON'T BE SURPRISED IF YOUR TEEN DOES WHAT YOU DO

I remember one mother who was greatly angered at one of my evening parent talks. I could see her approaching me from fifty feet away with her fists clenched and purpose in her fast-paced steps. Trying to justify her actions, she started right in on me. "So you are trying to say that if I stop drinking alcohol, you can guarantee me that my kids won't drink?"

I said, "I'm sorry, but you didn't hear me correctly. I never said that. I did say, however, not to be surprised if your kids end up doing as you have done."

Many have bought into a very popular cultural shift from "do what's right" to "don't get caught." As parents who are supposed to be living out the challenge of doing what Jesus would do, we have no choice but to live today as we want our kids to live tomorrow.

I've seen it happen time and time again. What parents do in moderation, their teen does in excess. It's not a hardened rule that always applies, but it happens too often to ignore. The parent (like the mother above) who drinks socially is surprised when her daughter becomes an alcoholic at nineteen. Or the father who has no other way to get through the weekend but to drink can't understand why his son was driving drunk and got killed. Alcohol and teenagers don't mix, and for them to drink is against the law. Just because society has moved from "don't break the law" to "don't drink and drive" doesn't mean you and I have to buy into it. There will never be a way to guarantee that our kids' lives won't be ruined because of alcohol—but there is a way to guarantee that they won't learn it from watching us.

Where do kids learn the most effective way to gossip? From us, of course. Any time we talk negatively about anyone—whether it be our boss or our pastor—our kids lock in on every word. Quite often they end up practicing this skill to the ruin of their own reputation. Kids aren't as careful or sneaky as adults (most adults who love to gossip don't have any idea that the rest of the world knows all about their favorite hobby), and therefore they gossip much more blatantly. I'm amused when I hear people say they have a hard time understanding Scripture, but I don't think we need to study Greek in order to clearly understand Titus 3:2: "They [God's people] must not speak evil of anyone."

Getting back to our parent-moderation leading to teen-excess theory, I've seen, as I'm sure you have, several other areas that seem to back this theory. The parents who watch R- and X-rated films are shocked to find pornography in their high school student's room. The father who says, "Tell the person on the phone I'm not here" is deeply hurt and angered when his twelfth-grader looks him straight in the eye and lies to him. The single mother who has no respect for her parents finds it impossible to believe that her own daughter is stealing from her. And of course the classic: The parents who cheat on their income tax go through the roof when their student gets caught cheating on a final exam.

BEING AUTHENTIC: TIME TO TAKE INVENTORY

Let me reaffirm that there is no evidence that shows our kids will imitate our actions 100 percent of the time. Quite often they will do the exact opposite. Just remember that no other human being on this earth will set the path for your children to follow like you will.

Let's take a look at several different areas to make sure that our actions back up our words. If my examples jog your memory about some other areas in which you need to align your walk with your talk, please jot them down in the margin.

Walking with God.

Is your spiritual journey going in the direction and at the speed you would like? Are there areas where your children are confused because of your hollow words? Are you willing to trust God with more of your problems after reading that section a few minutes ago? Does the amount of time you spend in prayer prove that you believe God has ears to hear and a heart that wants to help? Does your excitement about meeting God each day equal your enthusiasm if tomorrow morning you could meet with your favorite movie star? Most great sports stars had parents who made it a priority to practice with them, give lots of encouragement and praise, and spend lots of time watching their games. If we want our teens to be drafted into the big leagues with God, we must be authentic encouragers, or our words won't carry any weight.

Respecting people.

People are treated worse than animals in much of our world today. When millions are spent to save whales while unborn babies are legally slaughtered by the millions for the sake of convenience, our kids think this is the way life is and always has been. During their short lifetime and limited experience, they have seen few examples of people respecting each other. Be an example to your kids. Refuse to tear people down. Lift people's hopes and spirits whenever you are with them. The two people you should respect the most are (1) yourself and (2) whoever you are with. Look for ways to take care of both, every day.

Getting involved at church.

So many parents ask me why their teens won't attend the family church that it makes my head spin. I would have to say that this is the number-one area where hypocrisy is passed on to our kids. Parents who refuse to take an active role in their local church do just as much damage as those who become church-aholics. Taking your kids to church and dropping them off while you leave to do something more "enjoyable" shouts quite a message to them.

Have your kids kneel beside you while you pray for your church leaders and those having troubles. Don't forget to get excited about answers to past prayers as well. All in all, evaluate the role you play at your church and ask yourself if you would be pleased if your children did the same in a few years.

Respecting your mate.

One of the most damaging things we who are married can do is to put down our spouse in front of our children. Many parents seem to believe their kids are hard of hearing and have absolutely no perception. Sarcasm—anger expressed with a smile— is a chief weapon in this war. It may get something off our chest, but it does irreparable damage to our kids. Divorced parents, remember that your former spouse is still your child's parent and role model. Here especially, you must resist the temptation to tear that person down in front of your kids.

TODAY'S SEED . . . TOMORROW'S WEED

Anyone who has ever worked in a garden knows that weeds come uninvited and with great persistence. How many more weeds do you believe would pop up if we planted weed seeds? God tells us that children are punished for the sins of their parents to the third and fourth generations (Exodus 20:5). I have often wondered why I become easily angered or, at times, full of rage. I've discovered that this was a trait of my father and my grandfather. Neither one walked with the Lord, except my dad the last year of his life. He met Jesus at the age of seventy-six. I have had to work and pray very hard to overcome my outbursts of anger. Getting right with God and passing on a spiritual legacy is one of the greatest feelings a parent will ever know. As you cultivate the tender soil of your child's life, read the owner's manual very carefully to keep from planting the wrong kinds of seeds.

Obviously this can work positively as well. Today's seed can become tomorrow's gorgeous flower. When my son Brandon was five years old, I saw a classic illustration of this. We rode bikes together, and as we did, I called various neighbors by name, wishing one a good day and praising the next for his beautiful yard and so on. A couple of days later I was working in the garage and overheard Brandon saying the same things I had said, word for word. He even stopped his bike and, with one leg straddling the bar like me, stood on the sidewalk and shot the breeze for about three minutes with the same neighbor I did the day before.

I love how the apostle Paul had the confidence (in Christ) to tell us to live as he lived. He boldly says in 1 Corinthians 4:16, "I ask you to follow my example and do as I do." Our goal should be to have such a secure relationship with Jesus and an even greater desire to live a pure life that we can make the same statement to our teens.

WHAT ABOUT YOU?

1. What are you doing in moderation that your children could ruin their lives with if they took it to excess? Discuss with other parents habits that are accepted yet may be dangerous or damaging to your children if they follow your actions—things such as social drinking, gossip, laziness, a lack of love around the house, excessive TV time, or listening to any music without checking the lyrics.

2. Is there a support group or Christian counselor you could talk with to help you understand and overcome any destructive habits or patterns you may have that you aren't pleased with?

3. Would you be willing to ask your best friend or your children if you are saying one thing yet living out another? (Why does the mere thought of this scare us half to death?) What might we learn if a loved one would tell us the truth? Please don't let your pride keep you from changing for the happiness and good of your entire family.

4. What would have to take place in your life for you to have the desire to please God in everything you say and do? What would be needed to push you beyond the desire stage to the action

stage? Three things that will be of great help in this area are prayer, caring and supportive people, and a strategy to change given by someone who has successfully been there.

EXTRA POWER FOR PARENTS FROM GOD'S WORD

You can detect them by the way they act, just as you can identify a tree by its fruit. (Matthew 7:16)

A tree's water and nutrients go from the roots through the entire tree to bring forth the fruit that clearly identifies the tree for all the world to see. The world and our children see our fruit as well. The two main ways we exhibit fruit are through our *actions* and our *words*. What we *do* and what we *say* come from our *heart*. Do others know that we are in love with the Lord and desire to be pure in his sight more than anything else in our lives? And do we care enough about others to gently share Jesus with those who don't know of his love and forgiveness? It's time we stop being ashamed of who our Master Gardener is and what type of tree we are.

I, the Lord your God, am a jealous God who will not share your affection with any other god! I do not leave unpunished the sins of those who hate me, but I punish the children for the sins of their parents to the third and fourth generations. But I lavish my love on those who love me and obey my commands, even for a thousand generations. (Exodus 20:5-6)

Each of us will leave a spiritual heritage to our kids, whether we want to or not. God has a right to be jealous. He created us to give him glory. He even went so far as to send his Son to die in our place to seal the pact. If we will pass our love for him on to our children, we will be blessed now and they will have God's special blessings in the future.

> And now a word to you fathers. Don't make your children angry by the way you treat them. Rather, bring them up with the discipline and instruction approved by the Lord. (Ephesians 6:4)

I like the King James Version where it says "provoke not your children to wrath." It means to avoid severity, anger, harshness, and cruelty. Never punish when you are full of anger. It will come out as revenge. Instead, think in terms of correcting your kids with the affectionate concern of having them grow closer to God because of your actions. The second part of this verse tells us what to do instead of breaking our kids' spirit and driving them further from God. We are to nurture them with wholesome discipline and instruction, causing them to recognize these same traits when God disciplines them later in life.

> Listen, my child, to what your father teaches you. Don't neglect your mother's teaching. (Proverbs 1:8)

Each parent is to actively teach by word and example day in and day out. We instruct by our words, and we teach by our example. All eyes are on you. Your children are patiently waiting to see if you mean what you say and believe it enough to bother living it out yourself. This verse implies that parents know enough to seize every possible moment in training their children to learn God's ways throughout their lives. Notice that instead of *asking* parents to instruct and teach, God assumes we are *already doing it* and tells kids to pay close attention.

If your enemies are hungry, give them food to eat. If they are thirsty, give them water to drink. (Proverbs 25:21)

Why would I put a verse like this at the end of a chapter on parenting? Why talk about enemies? Simply because our kids learn more about us when we deal once with someone we dislike than by watching us around our friends one hundred times. At times, even family members treat each other like enemies. Those are precisely the times that our kids need our patience and calmness as if we were giving out food and water.

CHAPTER 4

We Do One Thing;
They Learn Another

JIM WAS one of the lucky ones. He could count on his mom and dad attending every high school sporting event he participated in. It might be two minutes before game time, but he would look toward the door of the gym if it were basketball, or the bleachers if he was playing baseball, and sure enough his mom or dad or both would be running in with excited expressions on their faces. He told me how important it made him feel, knowing that his parents took such great effort to arrange their schedules so they could watch nearly every competition of his three sports. He said it broke his heart to see fellow teammates search the crowds hopefully, yet seldom finding their parents. He said with confidence, "My parents attended my games, and I knew they did it because they loved me."

Bobby was in nearly perfect physical condition. He was the top wrestler in the entire state of Wyoming. He had received a full scholarship from a very expensive and prestigious university to show the world his God-given wrestling skills. As I stood with him on the front steps of his high school looking at his house directly across the street, my heart ached for him. I tried to crack a joke to lighten things up. "It must be hard to skip school living so close. I can't imagine you having a good excuse to be tardy."

With tears streaming down his cheeks he shared, "You know what really hurts? In my four years of wrestling here at this school, ending up the number one wrestler in the state, not once did my dad bother to cross the street to watch me. I know it's the alcohol—but it's just not fair. He robbed me of the joy of showing off in front of the most important person in my life. I don't know if I can ever forgive him, and it will take a long time for him to convince me that he loves me."

Two scenarios with opposite parental actions—each with a son trying his best to figure out how those actions relate to him. Jim saw his parents watching him and concluded that they must love him. Bobby, on the other hand, even though he knew his father's alcoholism kept him from public places, concluded that he wasn't one of the lucky ones who receive their father's love.

In the last chapter, we learned that kids hear best with their eyes. Our actions are the most effective teaching method we have. Unfortunately, we don't always realize just what message our actions are shouting. In fact, our kids quite often learn something entirely opposite from what we ever wanted to teach them. In this chapter, we'll look at some areas where we as parents may be sending messages to our kids that we are totally unaware of—messages that may well be exactly the opposite of the message we intended to send.

A COACH'S COMFORT ZONE

He coached a very successful Christian high school basketball team. There was one problem, however, and it seemed that everyone in the entire world knew about it—except him. The problem was that you couldn't tell he was a Christian. His actions were no different from those of any other successful coach, even those who didn't know Jesus. He would yell and scream to get his players' attention, then get totally frustrated if they goofed up a play or missed a shot. Several players never entered a game the first half of the season, even though many games were won by as many as twenty-five points. The straw that was about to break the camel's back was that he wouldn't pray with his players before and after each game as he was asked to do.

He said he wasn't called to be a preacher, and he had never been comfortable praying around others. He was a coach and felt the school should be happy because of his winning record. This was a classic case of an adult's doing something for what he felt was a very good reason, yet sending quite another message to all of the moldable young people watching his every move.

He said he wasn't a preacher, but his actions and words preached a very loud message. It went something like this: *You can be a Christian and never once mention your faith.* Young people conclude that you are ashamed of it or it simply isn't worth mentioning. Screaming and getting angry at a player's best efforts, as well as refusing to let everyone play, sends the message that winning is the most important goal. And the loudest statement made by this coach's actions was that it's OK to be a Christian role model in the lives of fifty teens for four years and not lead even one of them any closer to Christ than they were when they started.

Over the past twenty years, the thousands of teens I've talked with and received letters from have helped me identify three different ways parents confuse kids and send the wrong messages. We as parents send mixed messages by not doing the right thing, by doing the wrong thing, and by not doing anything at all.

NOT DOING THE RIGHT THING

Quite often we fail to do what is right—as well as what is expected of us—because we lack faith in God's promises, protection, and plan for our lives. As we look at a couple of examples, remember that God can only be the master chess player and put Satan in check if we allow him to move us where and when he desires.

Teenage booze party.

This happens every weekend in America. A teen goes to a beer bash. His parents know about it and say nothing. What does this simple action—not doing the right thing—say to the teen? It says that they care very little for the child's safety. This failure to act also shouts that we have little respect for the law or the police. Young people tell me they wonder why their parents don't challenge their actions when they are breaking the law.

Alcohol-related traffic accidents are still the number one killer of teens. If we stand by and fail to call the police when a party is in action, our teens will have little reason not to go along with the crowd. Peer pressure has won again. We must not let this happen. Find out about each and every party that your teen attends. Who is in charge? Get to know the parents if at all possible. Have your teen come into your bedroom when he or she returns, so you'll be able to smell any evidence of alcohol or marijuana use. Kids will respect you for it, and you might be saving their life.

But he is our favorite!

It was a classic case of parents who were afraid to critique or discipline their famous sports-star son. He was the oldest of three boys, the most popular at school, the best athlete, and the rudest and most disrespectful person in the house. How could both parents look the other way while taking the verbal abuse he dished out? They thought they were simply being kind to their favorite son, but in reality they were teaching lessons that would come back to haunt them someday.

Many hidden messages are picked up and stored by the children in a home where favoritism is displayed. The boy who seems to be the winner now will expect the rest of the world to bow every time he enters a room or demands attention. Reality won't hit until he receives a "parent-ectomy" upon graduation and moves out on his own. The problem with crippled kids such as this, however, is that they usually plan on staying home until they are about thirty years old. If I were him, I would like to stay there too!

The other siblings learn lifelong lessons as well: (1) It's normal to play favorites. (2) Some people are above rules and laws. (3) It's normal to be a people pleaser. The confusing part of all this for these unfortunate siblings is that no one ever explains how we are to choose who gets treated specially and who doesn't. They learn to hate the favored sibling and their parents, and someone needs to warn their future spouses and children.

Please treat everyone in your home by the same standards—especially when it comes to administering discipline. As we mentioned earlier, a life without regret is worth anything you have to do to achieve it. Start today to teach that every person in your family is a miracle sent from heaven and deeply needed to turn your house into a loving home.

A little white lie.

Never model a lie for your kids, even in saying that you aren't home when a phone call is for you. We may have a legitimate reason for not wanting to talk on the phone after a long hard day, but we need to express it honestly. Lying about not being home teaches our kids that some lies are OK, and that there are certain times in our lives that lying is an appropriate solution to a problem. Since lies are the number-one way of breaking trust between a parent and teen, commit yourself to God right now to never again tell any lies. You will be sending a message to your teens that they will never forget. You won't even have to tell them about your pledge to God! Before too long, they will sense your stand for truth.

We tell small lies in many other forms as well. Gossiping, breaking promises to God or others, fooling ourselves by pretending we don't have a certain problem or need for help, and exaggerating to make stories more interesting are just a few of the ways we model lies in front of our kids. (Oh, that last one hurt! Being a motivational speaker, I have to work very hard not to jazz up my stories by making them bigger than life.)

DOING THE WRONG THING

Doing the wrong thing is obviously very closely related to not doing what is right. I want to point out in this section some very common actions and statements that should be avoided at all cost. Whereas failing to do the right thing often stems from a lack of faith that God will see us through it, doing what is wrong is often rooted in ignorance. Be blind no longer.

She sure is beautiful!

Many teens are devastated when they hear their parents admire another young person's beauty, talent, or intelligence. Most parents have no idea what goes through the mind of their insecure fifteen-year-old daughter when they comment on how attractive or thin one of her classmates is. You think

you are being nice and thoughtful by making a positive comment about one of her peers, but she feels you're saying that
you wish she were more like that other girl. In her mind, you
would love her more if only she looked or acted like the
person you are admiring. Remember how we learned earlier
that perception is everything, especially to teens? They will
probably never mention any of this to you. They will simply
wonder why you don't know what they are thinking.

Don't get me wrong. It's wonderful to express positive statements about others in front of your kids. It shows the nature of
God, whereas gossip and put-downs drive our teens the other
way. What I am talking about here is to be careful *what* you
notice in others. If your daughter can't duplicate the admired
quality, she will feel helpless and blame herself and God. Our
kids may never match up to another person's beauty, talent, or
intelligence. They are who they are, and God gives all of us
different abilities, looks, strengths, and talents.

Instead of admiring the star of the team while your son is
sitting on the bench, why not share how great it is that he has
practiced hard to make the most of his God-given talent. Then
take the opportunity to help your son find the areas he *can* excel
in. You will be showing your child qualities you admire as well
as leaving him with hope. There is no hope in trying to change
the unchangeable. By the way, your bench-sitter is really the
team member to be most admired. To work hard at practice and
not be allowed to play takes much more character and backbone
than being applauded for doing what comes easily, as in the case
of the naturally gifted superstar of the team.

Incidentally, while we're discussing comparisons, it won't
help the romance in your marriage if you mention how attrac-

tive another person's husband or wife is. There are definitely times to do as the great philosopher Ralph Kramden of *The Honeymooners* used to say: "Keep your mouth shut!"

I love you when you are perfect.

Many kids hear their parents' praise only when they have accomplished something great or acted perfectly. If the only hugs a teen receives come after the home run or straight A's, that teen will feel worthy of such affection only after an accomplishment. God has never put a condition on his love for us, and we have hurt him many more times than our kids have disappointed us. The Bible says he loved us while we were *still* sinning and that he loved us *way before* we loved him.

I experienced this type of "conditional love" when I was hosting *Straight Talk,* a teen TV talk show. I had to be perfect in order to hear any sort of praise. I would go through an entire episode doing everything I had planned, opening and closing each segment perfectly, going in and out of the audience with ease, asking all the right questions—and afterward the only thing the producers would comment on was that I had said "hot line" instead of "help line." Once I asked them why they never did anything to build me up and keep my enthusiasm high for the good of the show. My producers said, "We thought you were like Zig Ziglar, always positive, never needing any praise."

Many of us parents, myself included, treat our kids like this. It's time we wake up! We are losing the battle for our only future—our children. People are all the same inside, filled with feelings that need lifting and empty spots that need filling. Everyone needs appreciation and a feeling of importance to thrive. Without them it's a struggle simply to survive.

Tell your kids you love them because they are a gift from God. Hug them when they are feeling unhuggable. Never say—or even imply—that you love them more when they please you. (If you do, I strongly encourage you to notice how this might have been passed on to you from your own parents and to pray for the ability to break that destructive cycle. Never put conditions on the love you give away, especially to your kids.)

God intended our homes to be places where our kids can grow up in an atmosphere where practicing things is encouraged, not condemned or forbidden. I love to read about Thomas Edison's mother forever encouraging him to be all he could be. When asked who his greatest inspiration was he always mentioned his mother. He said she gave him the gift called "a love of learning." It's said that he made over ten thousand mistakes before he found the right material for the filament of the incandescent light. Perfectionists seldom make their world or anyone else's brighter, because they fear failure above everything else.

Jesus sent his disciples out two by two to spread the gospel. He told them to shake the dust from their sandals if they weren't received in love and to move on to the next town. He never graded their success by the number of converts but rather applauded them for their honest effort. Steven Spielberg's success has come about because he was encouraged to dream, reach out, try new things, imagine and develop a vision for the unseen. Our kids may never be famous movie producers, but they needn't have an unpleasant adulthood because we gave them messages that put conditions on our love.

What elephant?

No one ever wins when the truth is hidden. And when the hidden truth is dysfunction or abuse within the family, everyone loses. Family problems such as alcoholism, any type of abuse, workaholism, uncontrolled anger and rage, an affair, or out-of-hand troubles of any kind must never be ignored. Major family dysfunctions have often been described as a large, white elephant who sleeps on the living-room floor. Every family member has learned to ignore the huge family-wrecking intruder, to walk around it, and by all means to never mention it to anyone.

When a wife pretends that her husband is not an alcoholic and covers for him when he misses work or hurts her or the children, the kids learn lessons that will destroy their childhood and hopes for a peaceful life. They learn that the truth is to be avoided and troubles are to be sidestepped. Having never seen parents pray through problems, these kids learn that God is too weak or uncaring to help *our* family. They further learn that some problems are incurable and that they were simply too unlucky to be born into a happy home. What is even worse is growing up thinking that this kind of living is normal and then passing that crippled outlook on to their own spouse and children.

It's time to stop the treacherous trend that may have been passed down for generations. The truth will set you and every family member free from having to conceal this life-robbing secret any longer. Why not go to God right now in prayer? You may not have any of the problems I've described, but you are hiding your own white elephant—maybe even a couple of them. Give them over to the Lord, and if necessary, seek out professional Christian counseling. God has given you his promise that he won't walk away from you during your times of need. Turn to him. Trust him. Get support from a couple of strong close friends. Times like these give further evidence of the need for organizations like Promise Keepers for men and a strong, caring church home for both men and women. We each need a support network of intimate friends who will love us no matter what and desire our happiness as much as their own.

Whatever your support network is, tell them the truth about any problem that is stealing your family's joy and your deep desire to move beyond the pain. I realize I am asking you to do the most difficult thing you have ever been asked to do—but we both know that if this isn't dealt with today, it will be your home's constant intruder. Like a thief with an endless craving for your family's peace of mind, problems never retreat on their own. Let God help you take the first step today.

NOT DOING ANYTHING

Now that we have taken a look at some examples of not doing the right thing as well as doing the wrong thing, let's look at the easiest trap to get stuck in: not doing anything at all. Traditionally this has been known as "the sin of omission." We know what to do, but we simply choose to turn our heads and hope the problem will go away. As we look at our next three examples, notice how we paralyze our children instead of teaching them how to make godly decisions.

Not calling sin sin.

Their pastor was a gifted speaker. People from other churches came each Sunday to see if he was as marvelous an orator as they had heard. While outsiders envied this church for having such a great preacher, trouble was brewing within the church family. The shepherd was betraying the people and God by having an affair with his secretary. What was even worse was that the adults turned their heads from the problem and chose not to deal with it. It went on for several years, and no one confronted him or her, even though the church's life and witness were obviously eroding before everyone's eyes.

I wish this were an uncommon scene in churches today, but unfortunately it isn't. Many damaging messages came from the leadership's decision to stay quiet on this issue instead of dealing with it in love as Christ would have done. Many young people learned firsthand the wrong lessons: (1) Some positions of leadership are above the law. (2) It's good to go along with the crowd. (3) It's better to maintain harmony than to risk upsetting things by doing the right thing. The young people in this church were robbed of the opportunity to see men and women of God go to him in prayer, get convicted of their sin, and with the strength of the Holy Spirit, do something about a serious wrong.

This church is still staggering from that situation. When we know something is wrong—whether it be in our church, neighborhood, family, or school—we must act as Jesus would. Otherwise our kids will have no model to follow when God calls them to be light in the darkness. Choose always to act out what the Holy Spirit places upon your heart and mind. Talk it over with your kids, so they will know *why* you are doing what you are doing. Never let them assume you are acting out of pride when in fact the Lord has challenged you to make a stand for him.

It's a sign of weakness.
You may never have been taught to say this as a child. Neither was I. It was always regarded as a sign of weakness. Men especially avoided it at all cost. The Marlboro man never said it, nor did John Wayne. It would almost guarantee your being thought of as a sissy.

Have you guessed it yet? Actually many things could fit this description—anything that involves being willing to humble yourself before God, your spouse, and your kids. Each one of them takes more courage than doing nothing and letting bitterness harden into a lifestyle. Things like "I'm sorry," "Please forgive me," "I love you but don't know how to show it," "Will you help me be a better dad?" or "I guess I need God's help, too."

If these statements sound foreign to you, it's likely they were foreign to your parents as well. Give your kids a chance to see what the culture of our world knows little of—humbling oneself before God at the prompting of the Holy Spirit. Look at the wrong lessons you will be teaching if you refuse to act on God's whispered instructions to you: (1) Macho is in. Be tough at all costs. Big boys in this family don't cry. (Of course they don't live happy or fulfilling lives, either.) (2) Never share your true feelings with anyone because you might get laughed at. (3) Avoid being real, vulnerable, or pliable, no matter whom you could help if you would give it a try. (4) Who needs God? Shut off the message if he asks you to do something difficult or embarrassing.

Did you realize that you can actually save a life by asking someone's forgiveness? A sophomore wrote me the following letter:

Dear Bill,

After four years of rage and verbal abuse because of alcohol, my dad went to counseling. He was ordered to, or he would lose his driver's license. Mom and us kids didn't think he would stick it out. God must still be interested in us because my dad is a new man. He is kind and fun to be around just like when I was a little kid.

Last week he told me something that will deeply impact the rest of my life. It has even made me want to go to church and read my Bible more. It may sound simple to you, but it has given me hope for our family and my own life. My dad cried in front of all of us and asked for our forgiveness for the pain he caused over the last few years. When he looked me in the eye and said, "I'm sorry," I put my arms around him and told him, "I forgive you, Daddy, and everything will be OK."

I have never felt so needed or important in my entire life. Please tell other parents that they don't have to be superhuman, and when they make mistakes, as we all do, to simply say, "I'm sorry." It works miracles!

Signed, Happy Again

He might get a big head.

Both parents walked up to me after my talk. Before they even shared one word, their distressed looks told me they had a serious problem. Their sixteen-year-old daughter had recently been hospitalized for an attempted suicide. During counseling, they found out that their daughter was crying out because no one ever made her feel special. The dad told me that the way he was raised taught him that compliments would only give someone a prideful attitude and a big head.

Show me the person, especially the uncertain adolescent, who doesn't need ongoing encouragement and reassurance, and I will show you a hardened fool. Pats on the back and cheers from significant people rally each of us to do our best for ourselves, our loved ones, and our God. Ignoring teens will only drive them to do something noticeable. We each strive to understand our significance to our family as well as our place in this world. If our parents don't make us feel important, needed, and wanted, we will search out the person, group, or gang that will.

My close friend Jacob Aranza tells of meeting a teen in England who had a multicolored Mohawk haircut. It was held up by superglue! Jacob asked him, "Why do you choose to have your hair look like this?" The boy simply responded, "I'd rather be looked *at* than looked *over.*"

I found this anonymous poem that challenges me to remember to bring out the specialness in my children at all times.

The Average Child

I don't cause teachers trouble
My grades have been OK.
I listen in my classes
And I'm in school every day.

My teachers think I'm average
My parents think so too.
I wish I didn't know that
Cause there's lots I'd like to do.

I'd liked to build a rocket
I have a book that tells you how,
Or start a stamp collection
Well, no use in starting now.

'Cause since I found I'm average
I'm just smart enough you see,
To know there is nothing special
That I should expect of me.

I'm part of that majority
That hump part of the bell,
Who spends his life unnoticed
In an average kind of hell.

WHAT ABOUT YOU?

1. What are you doing that might convey to your children that you love something more than them?

- Do you read the paper when they want to talk? If so, what message are you sending?
- Do you find yourself watching TV when you could be having family time together?
- Does your favorite sport or hobby take large amounts of time away from your chores, responsibilities, or family?

Many times single parents spend so much time with their new girlfriend or boyfriend that the kids not only have to deal with the divorce but now wonder why the new friend is loved more than they are. While having a social life of your own is important as we discussed in chapter 2, please don't let your kids come in last place when you are struggling for your own feelings of importance. Similarly, I've talked with many parents who are going back to college, and they are amazed that their teens are getting into so much trouble with all the free time available to them. I remind them that their child will be leaving the nest soon, so enjoy them while they are still at home. Maybe your education can wait another couple of years.

2. What sins of omission are you committing simply because you are afraid of the truth?

- Are you covering up your spouse abuse or alcoholism?
- Are you telling lies to keep your teen out of trouble?
- Are you looking the other way when you suspect your daughter is sleeping with her boyfriend?
- Do you think your son's bad friends will go away if you just pray hard enough?
- Are you afraid that the truth about your family's troubles will be the latest topic for gossip?
- Whom can you talk to who has confronted a problem and has a much stronger and happier family because of it?

Get whatever help you need to confront your elephant with the truth!

3. If you were to ask your children which of your activities are taking time away from them, what would they say?

4. Is it easier for you to react out of anger or respond in love?

5. Do you speak what you're thinking instead of thinking before you speak? If so, what message are you sending your kids? Is it giving glory to God? What would it take for you to change before you have more regrets?

EXTRA POWER FOR PARENTS
FROM GOD'S WORD

> About that time David's son Adonijah, whose mother was Haggith, decided to make himself king in place of his aged father. So he provided himself with chariots and horses and recruited fifty men to run in front of him. Now his father, King David, had never disciplined him at any time, even by asking, "What are you doing?" (1 Kings 1:5-6)

David was your basic absentee father. By choosing to say nothing when his son decided to make himself king, he put lots of people in danger for their very lives—even Adonijah himself. Solomon was supposed to be king and would have missed out on his chance if Nathan the prophet had not spoken up when he did.

As parents, we are to act as protective umbrellas guarding our kids from Satan's attacks. When they step out from underneath our protection (and they will, if we shirk our responsibilities as David did!), Satan's deadly spears, like raindrops, have nothing to stop them. Speak up at all times when your kids need your advice, thoughts, prayers, or clearly spelled out rules.

I am the one who corrects and disciplines everyone I love.
(Revelation 3:19)

Don't ever promise to follow through and then not do it! Kids feel like they are left out in the cold without parents who care when they have no stability or structure in their lives. I tell teens that they are fortunate indeed if their parents have what it takes to say no. If you have a feeling (or know for sure) that your teen will be with the wrong people, at the wrong place, doing wrong things, please speak your mind and heart and do something about it.

Many parents wish with all their might that they had taken a stronger stand when they had the chance. Hundreds of teens tell me face-to-face, as well as in their letters, that they would give anything to have a parent who would explain the rules, set tougher standards, and then back them up with the proper discipline once they disobeyed. Young people become drunk with confusion when parents present no guardrails along life's treacherous curves. God cares enough about us to tell us when he disapproves of our actions, and we should do no less for our kids if we love them as we say we do.

He noticed a fig tree beside the road. He went over to see if there were any figs on it, but there were only leaves. Then he said to it, "May you never bear fruit again!" And immediately the fig tree withered up. (Matthew 21:19)

We learned earlier that a tree is known by its fruit. The world can tell a lot about us by watching and listening to our children. If we don't live out God's best in us as examples for our kids to live up to, God may allow our believability to wither away as he did the fig tree because it failed to bear fruit.

It's very interesting to realize that in the verse just before this one Jesus was hungry. The fig tree failed to provide the fruit it was meant to produce. God plans for our children to carry the message of the gospel throughout the world. How can they, if we do what is wrong, avoid what is right, or let our teens go their own way without training them as best we know how?

> So if you are standing before the altar in the Temple, offering a sacrifice to God, and you suddenly remember that someone has something against you, leave your sacrifice there beside the altar. Go and be reconciled to that person. Then come and offer your sacrifice to God. (Matthew 5:23-24)

Our attitudes toward others reflect our relationship with God. Our teens see us looking good at church but refusing to heal their broken hearts with extra hugs when we are angry and have hurt their feelings. Ask for forgiveness for broken promises, hurt feelings, insensitivity, or failure to humble yourself when God wanted you to. Each day we should get on our knees and ask God to pour out his Holy Spirit upon us and our family and to give us favor with our children. God loves to honor parents who desire only his best for their kids.

CHAPTER 5

How Valuable Are Your Values?

HE WAS a very caring and wise high school principal. I had just finished an exhausting day at his school. I asked him if he ever gets shocked by the things students or parents do, after being in education for over twenty years. He said it's been awhile since he has been totally thrown for a loop, but people's actions still shake him up from time to time. Here is one gripping story he had to tell.

A beautiful high school girl was found weeping profusely while lying in a fetal position in a corner of the girls' locker room. She was talking about committing suicide because she feared her parents' reaction to her being pregnant.

By four o'clock that afternoon the principal had both parents and the daughter in his office. He asked the parents some questions before he told them why they had been called to the school. "Do you love your daughter more than anyone you know in your neighborhood?"

With perplexed looks, both the parents said yes.

The principal continued, "Do you care more about your daughter than all the people and opinions put together at your church?"

"Why, yes," came their second reply.

"What about all the people where both of you work?"

"Of course we do," they affirmed, "but what is all this about?" Then the principal proceeded. "Your daughter needs you both very much. She needs your love and understanding today more than she has ever needed it in her sixteen years. She wanted to kill herself this morning because she thought you would explode if you knew she was pregnant."

The parents realized in those few minutes how important their daughter was to them. The principal had asked those questions to get the parents to focus on the things they value most, and off the people who may think less of them or their daughter because of her pregnancy. Along with their daughter, they went through counseling, worked with a Christian adoption agency, and helped pick out a home for her baby a few months later.

This chapter will be much easier on you than that meeting was on those parents, and you will still come out with a list of the things you value most in your family. Within the next few minutes you will be able to do what 90 percent of your friends have never done. You will identify the top ten values you want your kids to carry with them throughout their lives and write them down for each family member to see.

YOU CAN'T GIVE AWAY WHAT YOU DON'T OWN

Just as you can't give away your neighbor's lawn mower, you can't pass on his values to your kids. They must be yours. Those values must be bought with a price, or they won't stand up against the political correctness of our day. Let's face reality. Believing in strong Christian ideals can cause a person to lose more friends than having bad breath. With all the talk about family values today, our kids have totally tuned those words out. If they aren't identified, talked about, and given as high a place of importance as your new golf clubs, you can forget about your teens having a desire to live them out.

Picture this. Your youngest child is in his twenties and writes you the letter you have been dreaming of for years. In this masterpiece that many parents are fortunate enough to receive, you are thanked for all the things you did right. He appreciates the times you had to stick to your guns and enforce the rules. He goes on and on about how wonderful your walk with God is and the security he felt throughout his childhood because of it. To be able to talk to you about anything without being laughed at is a skill you passed on to him that will help ensure his successful marriage. By making him stick to commitments such as Little League and his paper route you have passed on a work ethic that few of his friends know anything about. He goes on for two wonderful pages. As you wipe away the tears, you read his PS: "Most of all, Mom and Dad, I want to thank you for . . ."

What would you want the last sentence to say if you were reading that letter from your child? If you were to list ten things, you would have the ten main values that you want to see lived out in your kids.

Many people never write out their values because they want to wait until they have time to come up with the "perfect" list. They become paralyzed, and it never gets done. Remember, this can be a working list. You can change or add to the list whenever a new or important value is desired by a family member. So just get started and see what you come up with.

As you think about identifying your top ten values, keep in mind the things that were a part of your childhood that are so obviously missing today. What are young people in want of that drives them toward a life of crime and gangs? What values will ensure that your kids feel accepted, needed, important, and deeply loved? As you identify your values in a few moments, make sure they will give your kids a glimpse of the character and glory of God.

If your kids are old enough to sit through a short family meeting, they can help you decide on the main values you all want to live out and be known for. I want to show you the list of ten that my family is using. Use any of these you wish and add to the list or rephrase them if it will work better for you.

1. **Honesty:** We must tell the truth and be honest with each other at all times.
2. **Trust:** We can trust one another in this family. We must work at it daily.
3. **T.U.A.L.:** We offer each other Total Unconditional Acceptance and Love. We love and accept one another with no strings attached. Performance and obeying the rules will never be a condition for our love and acceptance of one another.
4. **God is our friend:** God is our friend and can always be trusted to lead each of us in the best direction for the good of our family.
5. **God's ways are always best:** God will always be wiser than we are. We need to study the Bible to find his directions for our lives.

6. **Pray together:** Families that pray together stay together. We must never hesitate to pray with each other. It will keep us close to each other and God.

7. **Family time:** Since love equals time spent with each other, we must make it a priority to spend lots of time together enjoying each other's company. [We have committed to spend all vacations together, at times bringing a friend along. We try hard not to let the TV and other activities keep us apart.]

8. **We protect each other:** Kids stand up for each other at school and in front of friends. We protect each other with our words and would be willing to die for one another.

9. **Forgiveness:** We each realize how much God has forgiven us. Therefore we freely forgive one another and pray for God's help and strength to always do this.

10. **Talk it out:** We can talk about anything around here. Any person can call a family meeting at any time to openly discuss anything important to them. We are strong believers that the truth will always be better than pretending there are no problems.

Well, there you have my list. Now it's time for you to get your family's list of valuable values on paper. I've even supplied the paper. Remember that these can be changed at any time. What's most important right now is to get them written down. In our next chapter you will discover a technique that will allow you to see if your values are being upheld and put into practice each and every day.

Our Family's Top Ten Values

1.

2.

3.

4.

5.

6.

7.

8.

9.

10.

WHAT ABOUT YOU?

1. Why do you feel most people have a hard time identifying their values?

2. Why is it so easy to follow society and take on its values as your own?

3. What other families have values similar to yours? It would be a wonderful encouragement to talk with them about the things that are near and dear to your heart. Share your values with them and have them do the same with you. Pray for strength for each other in never compromising your values in our valueless society.

4. When the principal met with the parents of the pregnant teen, do you think he asked the right questions? Did he have any right to interfere in this situation? How would you have responded? What would you do if your daughter were pregnant or contemplating suicide?

5. What values do you feel your parents grew up with that your kids will not inherit unless you make them a priority?

EXTRA POWER FOR PARENTS FROM GOD'S WORD

The king of Assyria then commanded, "Send one of the exiled priests from Samaria back to Israel. Let him teach the new residents the religious customs of the God of the land." So one of the priests who had been exiled from Samaria returned to Bethel and taught the new residents how to worship the Lord.

But these various groups of foreigners also continued to worship their own gods. In town after town where they lived, they placed their idols at the pagan shrines that the people of Israel had built. (2 Kings 17:27-29)

Notice that these new settlers were taught about the Lord but only wanted him to be one of their good-luck charms—just like many people today. They will obey God if it doesn't interfere with the way the world views them. Any god that happens to be politically correct will do until a fresh, new one comes along. Pray with all of your might never to fall into the morally corrupt quicksand that swallows up those who keep one foot in the world and the other in God's Word.

> No one can serve two masters. For you will hate one and love the other, or be devoted to one and despise the other. (Matthew 6:24)

Jesus made it clear that heavenly values are in direct opposition to earthly ones. You can always tell if God is your Lord—rather than materialism or worldly things or philosophies—by asking what occupies most of your time, thoughts, and energies. Put God and values that will honor him and draw your kids closer to him in the center of your home.

> O Lord, you alone are my hope. I've trusted you, O Lord, from childhood. (Psalm 71:5)

The psalmist was old and looking back at his life as a testimony of all that God had done for him. In this day of fear and uncertainty for most young people, wouldn't hope be a great gift to pass on to your children? By listing our ten most important values, we may be blessed someday to hear our kids quote this psalm and truly mean every word of it. What a gift that would be!

> If you try to keep your life for yourself, you will lose it. But if you give up your life for my sake and for the sake of the Good News, you will find true life. And how do you benefit if you gain the whole world but lose your own soul in the process? (Mark 8:35-36)

God isn't saying here that our lives are useless. He's merely trying to show that nothing, not even our life, can compare to the riches of living for Christ. By establishing and maintaining family values, we will be helping our children desire to follow God instead of searching for self-satisfaction their whole life. Our kids see many examples of successful people who have traded God's approval for worldly success. Values help people aim at the right target.

CHAPTER 6

Put Your Values to Work

SHE WAS as wise and persistent as any parent I had ever met. She told me her story as the last few families were leaving at the end of my seminar. My kids weren't quite teenagers yet, so I listened with extreme interest.

When her daughter was twelve years old, this mother had said, "You can call me any time of the day or night if you are being asked or forced to do anything you think is wrong or choose not to do. I promise I will come and get you, no matter where you are or what time it is. I also promise not to ask any questions. I just want to bring you home safe and sound."

The mother shared how she had reinforced this message by telling it to her daughter many times each year throughout junior high and high school. "She is now twenty years old. Two months ago she called me at two o'clock on a Saturday morning. She sounded distressed and out of breath. She said, 'Mom, do you remember your promise?' I said, 'Where are you, honey? I'll be right there.'"

"Where was she, and what happened?" I anxiously asked this precious mom.

With tears in her eyes, she continued her story. "She was at a motel two hours away in the town where she goes to college. Her boyfriend had decided this was the night she should have sex with him. Once at the motel, he gave her the choice of sleeping with him or walking home. She knew she would not have to walk home! As I drove her home, she thanked me for reminding her year after year of my promise, because without it she might have given in to him."

At this point she was nearly overcome with emotion. She composed herself and went on. "In the two months since that night, we have become closer than we were even when she was a little girl. We totally trust each other with anything we need to share. It's all because she was able to remember in the heat of the moment what I said and what our family stood for. Most girls give in to their boyfriend because they don't want to lose him. Many won't call their parents because of fear that they will blame them for getting into the situation in the first place. I'm just so glad I kept telling her to call all those years. Can you believe it? God allowed me to help save my little girl from making a big mistake."

This mom—and her story—moved me beyond words. Success stories are rare in my line of work.

This mother did exactly what I would love for you to be able to do after reading this chapter. She reinforced her family values year after year, maintaining a friendship with her daughter that made her believable when she said, "Call me if you ever need me." Some of her values were honesty, trust, open communication, and keeping promises. She followed through by driving two hours to pick up her daughter and letting her tell her side of the story. We are about to discover a simple way of putting our values to the test anytime we choose.

OUR FAVORITE TOOLS ARE USED OFTEN

If we will work hard to put our values to the test daily, they can be the emotional and spiritual glue that holds our family together. Values lived out by loving parents are like little unseen threads that hold a piece of fabric together—unseen to an outsider, but giving strength to the family, security to the kids, and a sense of confidence and stability to the parents. Just as we keep our favorite gardening tools within easy reach on the workshop wall, we need to have our values hung clearly on the walls of our minds and hearts so they are within easy reach.

It's very important to take healthy pride in putting your values to work, as we are going to learn in this chapter. It's OK—in fact, it's absolutely vital—that we parent from a position of strength. Just as the great Sherlock Holmes would continually be on the lookout for any clue that could help him solve the case, we must pray for a keen sharpness in spotting ways to put our values to work—opportunity parenting. Let's look at two steps that can bring our values to life in a way that our kids will never forget.

> *Step 1:* Look for teachable moments throughout the day.
> *Step 2:* Ask yourself, How can I reinforce one of my values by my response to this situation?

These two simple steps can revolutionize the way you parent as well as the effectiveness you bring to the job. That is, of course, if—and I do mean a great, big, emphatic *if*—you remember them.

As we look at several situations that can, and usually do, pop up when we least expect them, try to *notice the opportunity* that has just landed in your lap (step 1), and then ask yourself the question, How can I reinforce one of my values by my response to this situation? (step 2).

Let's quickly review my family's list of top ten values. We'll be using them in the examples that follow.

1. **Honesty:** We must tell the truth and be honest with each other at all times.
2. **Trust:** We can trust one another in this family. We must work at it daily.
3. **T.U.A.L.:** We offer each other Total Unconditional Acceptance and Love. We love and accept one another with no strings attached. Performance and obeying the rules will never be a condition for our love and acceptance of one another.
4. **God is our friend:** God is our friend and can always be trusted to lead each of us in the best direction for the good of our family.
5. **God's ways are always best:** God will always be wiser than we are. We need to study the Bible to find his directions for our lives.
6. **Pray together:** Families that pray together stay together. We must never hesitate to pray with each other. It will keep us close to each other and God.
7. **Family time:** Since love equals time spent with each other, we must make it a priority to spend lots of time together enjoying each other's company.
8. **We protect each other:** Kids stand up for each other at school and in front of friends. We protect each other

with our words and would be willing to die for one another.

9. **Forgiveness:** We each realize how much God has forgiven us. Therefore we freely forgive one another and pray for God's help and strength to always do this.

10. **Talk it out:** We can talk about anything around here. Any person can call a family meeting at any time to openly discuss anything important to them. We are strong believers that the truth will always be better than pretending there are no problems.

Situation 1: Your sixteen-year-old son gets caught telling a lie.
Lies tear apart trust in families. Without forgiveness and the ability to forget, lies ruin relationships. Your response in this situation will do more than just reinforce one or more of your values; it may save a multitude of future heartaches. Once you realize you have an opportunity to reinforce a family value, look at your list of values and ask yourself which ones you can reinforce here, and how. It's often helpful to think about how Jesus would respond.

Your son has violated value #1, honesty. When honesty is violated, then value #2, trust, is also affected.

When we ask which values we can reinforce with our response and consider what Jesus would do, #9 (forgiveness) and #10 (talking things out) seem like a good place to start.

First we would sit down, and I would encourage him to tell his side of the story (#10). Calmly talking this through will make it easier for us to talk the next time a problem arises. Next, I would pray with him (#6) and tell him that just as God has forgiven me (#4 and #5) for the times I lied to him, I also pass that forgiveness on (#9).

Can you see how this two-step formula almost assures you that harmony is maintained in your home? Without a formula or plan it would be very easy to lose your cool—and along with it, any chance of using this as a teachable moment. By applying different values to difficult situations we turn potential trouble into opportunities. That's what opportunity parenting is all about. We remain in control instead of allowing awkward moments to disrupt the love we have for each other.

It's important to notice that I didn't harp on the fact that my son lied and broke our trust. He knows that. He was caught telling a lie, and if I throw it back in his face in anger, I'll simply make things worse and almost guarantee that he won't see the nature of God in me. Nor will he ever want to talk with me about future troubles.

Situation 2: Your sixteen-year-old daughter wants to date a twenty-year-old guy with a reputation for selling drugs and sleeping around.

I thought you might be dozing off on me and felt the need to catch your full attention!

Because of your daughter's age, this one must be handled with extreme caution. Many parents have overreacted in similar situations and driven their daughter out of the house and into the guy's arms. Remember step 1: Realize that this is a teachable moment, a time to communicate and grow closer to each other as well as to God, not a time to let Satan have a victory. This is a great opportunity to put your values to work, but definitely not a time to react out of anger or try to control her as if she were a little child.

The next step is to let values #8, 10, 5, and 7 come to the rescue.

Value #8: We protect each other. Share that you only want to protect her from a potentially dangerous and damaging situation. This is a situation where experience would be a terrible teacher if the lesson to be learned was endangering her life with sex or drugs.

Value #10: Talk things out. After listening to her side of the story, talk to her and take her to other girls who will tell her straight out what a twenty-year-old guy with a reputation like that is really interested in. Find other girls that your daughter looks up to and respects. Then have the boy come over to your house for an open discussion of his reputation, his desires, and your concerns. You will find out exactly what type of character he has.

Value #5: God's ways are always best. God wants us to associate with people who are believers in Christ as we are. Of course, I'm assuming your daughter has chosen to follow Jesus. If she hasn't, share with her how God desires only her safety and the best for her future. The important thing here is to realize that your calmness will help her desire your God and his forgiveness, rather than driving her further away.

Look up some verses that will clearly show it is God's will for your daughter to protect her reputation, to avoid putting herself in compromising situations, to obey your wishes for her, and to honor him through her dating relationships. For example, 2 Corinthians 6:14-18 tells how we should date other Christians. Philippians 4:13 shows how God can give us strength to obey him in all things, including our dating life. James 4:4 can be used to challenge her to never compromise her beliefs or values on a date. Proverbs 7:6-21 describes the glamour of sex leading to sin. Many more verses can be found relating to obeying God and parents. It's very rewarding to search God's Word with a son or daughter, looking for verses that pertain to their specific dilemma. They will never forget this time together or the verses you find.

Value #7: Family time. There is usually a reason teens rebel and desire to go against your wishes. There is probably a root problem that this daughter is crying out for help about. By spending time with her and giving her lots of attention, quite often you will win her back to your loving affection. In any situation like this, pray as if your child's life depends on it. It may!

We just took a very difficult and demanding situation and acted with wisdom and a plan, instead of causing potentially permanent damage to the relationship. By applying our two steps we were in control, rather than letting the plight that was before us take over and dictate our response. There is no guarantee about how your daughter will respond, but you will have assurance that you are acting lovingly and wisely. Let's take a look at another situation.

Situation 3: Your thirteen-year-old son is too shy to get involved in church, school activities, sports, or most social functions. All he wants to do is stay home alone.

Value #10: Talk it out. Be open with him about his strengths and the many blessings he possesses. It would be a wonderful exercise for him to list his many blessings and things he should be extremely thankful for. List his abilities one by one. Then add his friends, strengths, physical features such as eyes and ears, family, house, God's love, his forgiveness; continue until the list has thirty or forty items on it. It's very important for him to see how fortunate he is. Once people start noticing all the things they have going for themselves, it allows them to stop feeling insecure around others and puts their eyes on God and not on how wonderful everyone else seems to be.

Value #8: Protect him. You must protect him while at the same time gently forcing him to expand his comfort zone. While you should never force him into a situation where he could be embarrassed, you should not allow him to quit activities he has committed to. There are exceptions, of course. We went with our daughter as she finished each and every swimming and piano lesson she tired of soon after they started. But I did allow her, after much discussion and prayer, to call her cheerleading coach and back out of her commitment to the squad. She had worked hard to make the cheerleading team but later realized it just wasn't something she really wanted to do. I chose to look at this as a time to treat her as an adult and allow her to make the decision. It has encouraged her to come to me about any problem she faces. It is a real blessing from God when your daughter or son trusts you!

Value #3: T.U.A.L. The key to your son's feeling good about himself and trusting God for making him the way he did is for you to totally and unconditionally blanket him with your love. Never compare him to other, more outgoing kids. Pray hard that God will help you in this area if it's a problem for you.

Value #5. God's ways are best. God knew what he was doing when he made your son with his exact personality and strengths. He has a mission in life to glorify God in the way that God has chosen for him. Trust his plan for your son's life, and you will be passing that trust on to him.

Situation 4: Your fourteen-year-old son is depressed because a friend has moved away.

Once again, the solution to his problem is half solved once you recognize the opportunity to strengthen him by putting your values to work. Don't overreact. Time will heal this wound. Being careful not to belittle or make light of your son's feelings, you can assure him that things will work out.

Value #1. Honesty. Tell him that he will lose many friends throughout his lifetime. Some friends stop liking us. Some move away. As we get older, some get married and have different interests. Many teens have never been told what our grandparents knew: "This too shall pass." Speak the truth and prepare your kids for the hard times as well as the good times awaiting them. The truth will set them free from wondering why everything doesn't work out the way they had planned.

Value #7: Family time. This would be a great time to ask your son what vacation he would like the family to take this year. Let him get really involved in sending for brochures and making certain calls to plan out the details. It will keep his mind off his friend and show him how important family is. Take him out to dinner or to his favorite movie to help heal the immediate pain.

Value #10: Talk it out. After asking him to share his feelings with you, have him write his friend a letter telling how special the friendship is and that he wishes him the very best. He could offer to be a listening ear if his friend needs someone to write or talk to. You will be giving him a valuable gift—learning how to share his feelings—that he will be able to use throughout his adult life. This two-step process allows him to see that big boys do cry as well as talk and share and show the world that they are real.

Situation 5: Your daughter tells you she is pregnant.
What could be tougher than this? I would need to use every one of the ten values on my list in order to successfully help her get through this most difficult time.

Look over your list of ten values. Think through each one. Do you see how fortunate you are that she trusted you enough to tell you? Please notice that while she did make a very serious mistake that she will think about the rest of her life, she put the values of your family to work by not getting an abortion. (If she did get an abortion, she will need your open arms and silence to love her through this.)

Note that once again, we do not need to tell her about the mess she is in! That would only put a wall between us at a time when we need to be building bridges.

My dad taught me a saying that I use whenever any trouble hits, big or small: "If this is the worst thing that happens to us, we are going to make it." The pregnancy has already occurred. It's impossible to move back in time. Contact your local crisis pregnancy center and receive some valuable Christian counseling concerning your options.

I hope that you and I will never be faced with this—or many of these problems—but we both know that life and consequences are no respecter of persons. God is strong enough to help us get through any situation or trouble we find ourselves in. We must cling to God's hand as he walks us and our teens through the often dark and frightening forest life challenges us with. Keep your values in front of you and bring each one to life as you work through this character-building situation.

Situation 6: Your fifteen-year-old daughter has an eating disorder.

As you work through your values, please stay calm and try to see things from her perspective. When girls become anorexic or bulimic, they are crying out to a seemingly uncaring world that they are starved for affection and importance. As you read the following letter I received from a fourteen-year-old girl, look over your values and get prepared in case you are ever confronted with this problem.

> Dear Bill,
>
> I am bulimic. I feel so empty and lonely that I fill myself with food. After I binge, I force myself to vomit so I won't gain any weight. I have no boyfriend, and my family and I can't talk about anything. Why don't my parents love me? Why didn't God give me a happy home like all my friends have? I think about killing myself all the time. All I want is to be loved and needed by someone. Is that too much to ask?
>
> Thanks for listening.

That letter pretty much covers the main causes of eating disorders. These illnesses are cries for attention and love; the girls are letting people know they are unhappy and want to end their life. They must be treated with love and patience and usually professional Christian counseling. Earlier we talked about a teen's perception being reality, and nothing proves this more than teenage eating disorders. Put all of your values and your faith in God to the task of walking your daughter through this process of building up her life and self-worth.

Situation 7: Your teen refuses to talk to you about anything.
The key here is to recognize that a deeper problem has caused this. Most likely, we—as the communication teacher for the family—have failed to show *how* to talk things out.

There is no better time to start than now. Teens love attention! If you give them the time that you could be giving your work or hobby, they will know they are loved, and it will be much easier for them to talk things over with you. Think of how hard it is for you to share with a friend when he or she has slighted you or failed to come through for you.

I hope these seven examples give you a feel for using our values to turn a tragedy into a triumph. I find that I remember to act calmly when I am enjoying a close walk with God. When I have taken my mental, physical, and spiritual health for granted, I almost always ruin my chance to make God look good in the middle of a family crisis. However, when I am prayed up and listening carefully for God's still, small voice, I can usually teach a valuable lesson to my kids by applying the two steps we've been talking about. Give them a try and watch how much more laughter you bring into your home.

WHAT ABOUT YOU?

1. Why is it so easy for parents to react out of the feelings of the moment— yelling or passing on blame—instead of reinforcing an important family value?

2. What will you have to do to remember to think about your values and ask, "How would Jesus respond to this situation?"

when faced with a problem? Would it help to write your list of family values on a three-by-five card? You could easily refer to it throughout the day, and by carrying it around, you will have a better chance of thinking of it in the midst of a crisis.

3. How could an "encouragement team" of three or four couples play a part in your life?

4. Can you identify one or more of your values that you have failed to implement in your reactions to troubled situations? What can you do differently next time to handle the trouble with more patience and success?

5. Do you believe these statements?

- Values and morals filter down from the parents to the children.
- Kids watch and emulate their parents more than any other person.
- If you goof up, it's OK to forgive yourself, ask your kids' forgiveness, and start over.
- God has forgiven you for all of your parenting mistakes and never expected you to be perfect in the first place.
- With God at your side and in your heart, you can be the parent he wants you to be.
- With prayer as one of your strong family tools and your kids as friends, you can become a solid, loving family that sets an example for others to follow.
- No matter how bad things get, God has the answers and the strength to help you overcome any problems your family encounters.

- Our heavenly Father specializes in putting families back together.

I hope you believe all of the above statements. They are all true. God's Word and character back each of them up. God cannot and never will lie. He would never have allowed us to parent our children without first giving us what we need to do the job in a manner that is pleasing and honoring to him. Highlight these statements and claim them as your own every single day.

EXTRA POWER FOR PARENTS FROM GOD'S WORD

And you must commit yourselves wholeheartedly to these commands I am giving you today. Repeat them again and again to your children. Talk about them when you are at home and when you are away on a journey, when you are lying down and when you are getting up again. Tie them to your hands as a reminder, and wear them on your forehead. Write them on the doorposts of your house and on your gates. (Deuteronomy 6:6-9)

If you were to rewrite these verses putting the word *values* in place of *commands,* you would state the essence of this chapter in just a few sentences. God wants us to impress upon our kids that which is vitally important for their survival in a world that is betting against them. God isn't asking the youth pastor, the teacher, the neighbors, the coach, or anyone else to remind our kids throughout the day of his commandments. He is telling us, as their parents, to take advantage of every moment we are with our kids to teach godly lessons and reinforce our values.

> We are careful to be honorable before the Lord, but we also want everyone else to know we are honorable. (2 Corinthians 8:21)

Following the two steps in this chapter takes a constant awareness for disasters that can creatively be turned into victories. I love the way this verse challenges us to be honorable before both God and our family. Paul was talking about being above reproach when handling the money of the church. He took great precautions to be authentic as a preacher, and we can do the same as parents by taking great pains in responding positively to negative situations.

> You must worship Christ as Lord of your life. And if you are asked about your Christian hope, always be ready to explain it. But you must do this in a gentle and respectful way. (1 Peter 3:15-16)

This verse gives us a great road map toward our destination of teaching our kids with gentleness and respect. First we are to set our hearts up as a kingdom with Jesus on the throne. That makes him our Lord (the most important thing in the entire world to us). Next, we are to always be prepared to show our kids the control Jesus has over us by the calm way we apply the two steps in this chapter. I may have just paraphrased this verse, but nothing will make your kids desire a life dedicated to Jesus like your being totally sold out to him. The neat thing about these two steps as our plan of attack is that it's so easy to respond with gentleness and respect.

Don't forget, without these two steps, it's easy to let circumstances take over. With God's help our family values are powerful enough to carry us through anything that might come our way. Be on the lookout so you can put them to work!

CHAPTER 7

Nurturing and Teaching— A Season for Each

I'VE ASKED hundreds of parents if they feel the following true-life situation is a "teaching moment"—a moment in which to teach your teen a lesson that will never be forgotten. I'll tell you what they have told me over the years after you read the story and decide for yourself.

A seventeen-year-old son continued to defy his parents by hanging around with an eighteen-year-old guy who had a well-known reputation for using and selling drugs. This son was beginning to reap what his friend and he were sowing—bad grades and an attitude to match.

Late one Saturday night, the phone rang. In the presence of his parents, the son answered the phone. In shock, he dropped the phone and fell limply into a chair. A fellow student had just called to inform him that his black-sheep friend had died of a drug overdose earlier that evening.

Let's face it. This is a moment in which the teen is emotionally awake. Whatever his parents talk about or emphasize now, he will never, ever forget. So what would your answer be? Is this tragic situation a good opportunity for the parents to reinforce where they stand against drugs and questionable friends?

Most parents give the same answer that I thought for many

years was right—yes. And if you said yes, just like me, you are wrong. It took my sisters, Mary and Jean, to teach me otherwise. What they taught me in less than thirty minutes has revolutionized the way I parent and the love and friendship my kids now share with me.

When I shared the above story with my sisters and asked them if it was a time to teach a valuable lesson about drugs, Jean said, "Absolutely not! This is not a teaching moment, but rather a moment when *nurturing* is needed. What he needs right now— as well as in the days to follow—is your understanding, hugs, love, and acceptance. If you use this tragic time in his life to teach about the dangers of drugs, it will come across as 'I told you so' or 'Why were you so stupid not to follow my every command?'

"If he doesn't feel completely accepted and loved by you right now, he may never come to you again when troubles arise. He has just learned the truth about drugs from his friend's death. Don't imply that he is stupid by throwing the obvious back in his face. Hold him in your arms if he needs it, or respect his need to be alone if that's what he wants. Simply be there for him. Try as hard as you can to feel what he is feeling and go through it with him.

"When parents think only of their own agenda and use every possible opportunity to teach the lesson they hold so dear, often they end up showing a very uncaring response. Many children will shut them out emotionally, and it takes great effort to get them back."

As Jean talked, I could plainly sense God impressing upon my spirit that this was the area where I had gone wrong for so many years with my own children. I was always trying so hard to teach them right from wrong that I forgot how children feel, and I seldom made any effort to empathize with them when they goofed up or disobeyed me. I took all of my kids' actions personally. I thought everything they did was a reflection on me. If they were anything but perfect little adults, I was a complete failure! (Wouldn't you just love to be a four-year-old sitting next to me during a Sunday night church service?) Being a speaker and author on teen and family issues, I felt my kids should act and react perfectly. And I got very angry when they didn't (which, of course, was most of the time—so you can imagine how delightful it must have been to have me for a dad during those years). I was a codependent, only having a pleasant day if things and circumstances went my way or if people performed as I thought they should. Life is anything but wonderful when you demand what no person can ever live up to—perfection!

As both of my sisters continued to explain to me the difference between a nurturing moment and a teaching moment, I knew the direction God wanted for this book as well as for my life. He made it crystal clear that I was to write this book for myself, as I've previously said, and put its lessons to work in my own family in order to gain the peace I had previously searched for in all the wrong ways and places. I have since begun learning how to die to myself and have Jesus do, through and for me, what I haven't got the strength or wisdom to do myself—things like loving my kids when they disobey me, forgiving them when they act their age, enjoying them when they want me to get down on their level (even when I'm stressed out with problems of my own), and letting the past be the past, not bringing up dirty laundry whenever I feel like it.

Words could never fully communicate to you the freeing feelings I've had since my sisters opened my eyes to this wonderful discovery. I'm learning when to teach and when to reach out and be there for my kids; when to give information and when to simply listen to their hurt, pain, and confusion.

My goal is for you to have a close friendship and healthy bond with your teen. By understanding the difference between teaching moments and nurturing moments, you will be able to avoid the strained and explosive relationship that many teens and parents live with daily.

Let's look at some general principles concerning teaching moments and nurturing moments. Then we'll look at specific topics and when one is needed more than the other.

A TIME TO TEACH

Teach when they ask.

Possibly the greatest moment to teach our kids anything is when they come to us wanting the answer. These are rare moments indeed in teenagers' lives, as they are almost always smarter than their parents. But if such a rare occurrence does arrive, please find a quiet spot and answer their questions to the best of your ability. It's an honor when your teen comes to you for information that could easily be gotten from their peers.

Incidentally, teaching should always be age- and interest-appropriate. Only teach your kids what they need to know and what they can handle at their age. For instance, if your fourth grader asks about sex, tell him what he has asked for and leave it at that. Use appropriate terms and always tell the truth, but don't bore him with facts he isn't ready for.

Teach when opportunities arise.
These are teaching moments in the traditional sense. When your child goofs up, you can teach that it's not the end of the world. When he achieves something special, you can reinforce how his hard work paid off. When she loses a friend, you can share about how disappointing life—and friends—can be at times.

Opportunities don't have a good sense of timing, so you must be on the lookout at all times. From articles in the newspaper to graffiti on the bathroom wall at school, opportunities to reinforce your values abound if you will only keep your eyes and ears open.

Teach when good or bad things happen to other people.
When Magic Johnson retired from basketball because of the HIV virus, I sat my kids down and told them how he contracted the disease. It was a teaching moment, and I made the best of it to teach my kids the truth about sex outside marriage. When O. J. Simpson was on trial, we talked about the fact that he is either guilty or innocent. I shared that God knows the truth and that if O. J. did commit the crime, he will pay the price for his sins. Stories that catch your kids' attention happen every day. Use them to reinforce the lessons you want your children to know.

Teach when your child's emotions are aroused.
When your kids are happy, sad, glad, or mad, you have a chance to seize the moment and reinforce a lesson by using the emotion they are feeling to help the lesson stick. Remember, you can't teach anything to someone who is sleeping. But when the emotions are awake, the mind acts as superglue, ready and willing to catch any lesson you toss its way.

A TIME TO NURTURE

The key lesson about nurturing is this: When nurturing is needed, teens don't want to be taught anything! When kids are hurting emotionally, they want someone to listen and understand—not preach at them. If only parents could understand this lesson, fewer teens would run away from home. And many teens who are still at home physically would not be miles away emotionally.

Please try to be as sensitive as you can toward the moods of your teens. This is the first time they have ever been this age, and it is frightening them half to death. It's crucial that we refrain from losing our cool and raising our voice during nurturing times—times when our teens need our understanding and patience more than our advice. These are times when much prayer, wisdom, and patience are needed.

Even though we call these times "nurturing moments," they are moments in which our actions *teach* what is really important to us. Many teens learn much more about their parents during these unplanned times dealing with trials than they do from a lifetime of calm, objective teaching. When our kids need nurturing they are usually upset or frightened, and our proper response will enhance their self-worth and their confidence in their ability to handle future problems by themselves. At the very least, they will feel more comfortable coming to us for advice the next time they have the need.

Nurture when you have the desire to get angry.
Anytime we lose our cool, we are enacting a teaching moment whether we realize it or not. We teach our children that we can't stay calm when things go bad, or even worse, that God isn't big

enough to help us avoid stress during tough times. We also teach that it's better to come to us with good news instead of troubles. When we wildly react instead of gently responding, we teach many things that we don't really want to teach our teens. When it is tempting to point your finger and shake your child, please remember to seize the moment and not your teen. Nurturing can be very calming during trying times.

Nurture when your teen needs to get through a trouble or a trial.

The opening story of this chapter, about the friend who died of a drug overdose, is a perfect example of when nurturing is needed instead of teaching. These tough times are very critical because of the emotional nature of many teens. They will compare us unfavorably with their understanding friends if they fail to find loving support from us when troubles hit. Quite often they retreat to the friendly, open ears of their peers and avoid letting their parents know about any future troubles at all costs. Pray that God will be your strength and patience when times are at their toughest in your home.

Nurture when your teen disobeys or lies to you.

There are times, such as when your teen disobeys, that you will need to use two-thirds nurturing and one-third teaching. Your teen needs to realize that a rule has been broken and that discipline is needed, but that it will be handled calmly and lovingly. Try to look at things from your teen's point of view to better understand his or her way of thinking. The more patience you exhibit today, the more you will have for tomorrow. We'll look at some specific examples of disobedience—and the various ways you can respond—in the next chapter.

SOME DO'S AND DON'TS

As we look at several key issues and decide ways to teach and nurture in each of them, please keep in mind these do's and don'ts.

Do:

- Try to see things from their point of view. Try to feel the way your teen feels.
- Try to understand what your teen wants to express but can't find the right words for.
- Give your full attention to each issue your teen is concerned about.
- Pray for patience and ask your teen for help in understanding how he or she feels.

Don't:

- Overreact.
- Ignore problems and hope they will go away. (They will only grow if you are afraid to confront them in love.)
- Give punishment without discussion.
- Assume teens are the same today as when you were their age. (For that matter, don't assume anything!)
- Automatically think you know their feelings and hurts without asking them.
- Raise your voice.
- Let Satan drive a wedge between you and your teen over problems he wants you to think are insurmountable.

ALCOHOL, TOBACCO, AND OTHER DRUGS

How to teach.

Teach your kids how to say *never* to alcohol and other drugs. Back your words up with a lifestyle that matches. Expose advertisers and their true desire for money. Contact parents who are offering nonalcoholic parties for teens. Take a stand against alcohol whenever you can. Talk, talk, talk.

Everywhere you look someone has pain because of alcohol. The newspaper is full of tragic stories where lives are ruined because they were under the influence of teens' number-one drug of choice—alcohol. Cut out these articles and help your kids develop a deep-rooted hatred for this killer.

Don't laugh at booze commercials, and don't spend your precious time supporting such TV shows as *Cheers* that have a bar as their setting. Applaud actors and athletes who refuse to make money by endorsing beer commercials.

All of these suggestions are ways to teach our children that alcohol will always be our enemy and never our friend. There is obviously no guarantee that our teens won't drink even if we do everything possible to help them say no to it, but at least you will know that your words and lifestyle have not endorsed it.

How to nurture if problems arise.

Think ahead of time about how you would handle these situations:

- Booze or illegal drugs are found in your teen's room or car.
- Your teen is caught by the police at a booze party.
- Your teen comes to you with a drinking problem.
- Your teen steals money from you to purchase beer or cigarettes.

Parents who have a plan can better handle difficulties when they come up. Talk over all these possibilities with your teen and ask them for input as to how to handle these situations if they do happen.

GOD'S VIEW OF SEX

How to teach.

Most young people today know very little about God's view and purpose for sex. Teach your kids the truth, using the Bible as your source. (I would have no problem with our public schools teaching sex education if they would teach the truth and not distort it with their animalistic view of people.)

Genesis 2:24 teaches God's "leave, then cleave" plan: "A man [or woman] leaves his father and mother and is joined to his wife [or husband], and the two are united into one." Step 1 is to leave, or get married. Step 2 is to be joined (cleave), or have sexual intercourse within the bonds of marriage. Premarital sex replaces God's plan for our happiness and protection with pain, suffering, sexually transmitted diseases, and scars. God's policy is *never* to cleave first, then leave!

First Thessalonians 4:3-5 says, "God wants you to be holy, so you should keep clear of all sexual sin. Then each of you will control your body and live in holiness and honor—not in lustful passion as the pagans do, in their ignorance of God and his ways." Verse 8 gives each of us no excuse as to whom we are sinning against if we break God's sexual instructions: "Anyone who refuses to live by these rules is not disobeying human rules but is rejecting God, who gives his Holy Spirit to you."

Please help your teens learn these verses and understand that God wants only what's best for us. He is offering us his best advice so we can live a long, fulfilled life, full of peace while giving glory to him through our thoughts and actions.

Teach your kids that sex is much more than physical attraction. Like two rivers joining together, it is the merging of two souls. It is designed to unite a husband and wife into one. If it is done casually and without the commitment of marriage, it rips off a part of each soul when a person moves on to someone else.

If you were to put a piece of duct tape on your son's or daughter's arm and then rip it off, it would hurt and tear many hairs from their arm. If you did it a second time, it would pull only a few hairs off. The third time the tape would hardly stick at all. Sex outside marriage is like that tape on the arm. Duct tape is meant to hold two items together. Sex is one of the bonding agents that holds a marriage together. Once it becomes used with others outside of marriage, its godly purpose is diminished.

The truth will set you free. Be open and honest with your teens about your own sexual regrets and mistakes. Without unnecessary details, tell them your story. Many parents think that if they act like sex was not invented when they were teens, then their kids will listen to their advice. Nothing could be further from the truth. Keep talking and sharing about their sexuality. If you obeyed God and saved your virginity for marriage, tell how wonderful and free you felt because you did things God's way.

How to nurture if problems arise.
Every parent hopes and prays that no problems arise in this very delicate area. But real life obviously tells us differently.

Think and pray through how you would respond to an unwanted pregnancy. Seldom will your love and affection be needed more—and your "how could you?" and "why would you do this to us?" be needed less. Do you honestly believe God could help you through "Daddy, I'm pregnant" (or "My girlfriend is pregnant")? If you have any reservations about how you would handle a problem like this, please spend time with God and let him assure you that if you cling to him and allow his Holy Spirit to fill you daily, there is nothing you can't make it through.

What if your son or daughter contracts a sexually transmitted disease? Will you be there with faith and strength for your teen? Your understanding and love will never be more needed than during troubled times like these. As you wonder how to nurture when nurturing is needed, simply ask, "How would Jesus handle this?" Then stay calm and pray for God's strength to carry you through.

This is another area in which a delicate blend of teaching and nurturing will be needed. It's never too late to challenge a sexually active teen to turn that area over to God and start fresh. Help your teen make a vow to God that goes something like this:

> Dear God, I am so sorry for hurting you and others and myself with my selfish actions in my sex life. I want to start over and be clean in your sight. Please forgive me for my sins and renew in me a love for you and your Word. Give me a new appreciation for living in such a way that will make me never ashamed to be near you. From this day

forward I will save myself for my future mate. I love you and thank you for what you are about to do in my life. Amen.

My thirteen-year-old daughter, Emily, wears a "chastity ring." It is simply a reminder of her commitment to stay sexually pure before marriage. It has given her a chance to proclaim her beliefs to other students and friends when asked about it. It will, I hope, serve as a reminder throughout her dating years as well. She has told me of several times when she stood her ground against friends who made light of or bragged about the excitement of premarital sex. I'm convinced that our open discussions about God's plan for her sexually have helped her not to ever be ashamed of living to please him.

Volumes more could and have been written on this subject. Our purpose here is not to exhaust it but to give you a feeling for the difference between teaching and nurturing in this vital area. Your local Christian bookstore has many good books that you and your teen should read if you believe this area will be an extra temptation to your son or daughter. (See appendix C for a list of books to get you started.)

CHOOSING THE RIGHT FRIENDS

How to teach.
Never assume that your kids know what to look for in choosing a friend. Make a list of the character traits you want your kids to look for. Mention things that you want your own child to portray, because after a while they do take on the characteristics of their closest friends. Have them look for things such as being polite and honest, respecting others, being a good honest

worker, living out one's faith, and having good people skills. Reinforce how proud you are of them when they choose friends who will help them live out your family's values.

Try to understand why your teen is attracted to certain kinds of friends. If your children continually displease you, look deeper to find the root cause. Live out your own words by associating with friends who will take a real interest in your kids. This is one of the surest ways of helping your teen desire positive friendships. Reinforce your teaching by commenting on good and negative friends who influence others when you read about them in the newspaper or hear about them at school or in reports from neighbors and relatives. Use every possible teaching moment to back up your teaching on finding friends who will help your kids reach their true potential.

How to nurture if problems arise.
Being hurt or let down by a close friend is one of the toughest things teens go through. While it's part of growing up, the way you help them get through it will be a part of their bumpy or smooth takeoff into adulthood. Many teens have to weather this storm alone, leaving them bitter and afraid to enter close relationships for a long time to come.

In fact, as we were working on this book, my Tyndale House editor jotted the following note in the margin:

> Wow, I see now that this is what happened to me as a young teen. About the time my first "serious" boyfriend went off to college and ended up marrying someone else, my dad and mom were getting divorced and further break-

ing my heart. It took many years before I was willing to risk another emotionally intimate relationship.

You can help your kids avoid this pitfall. Share how you have been hurt and how people have let you down or stabbed you in the back. Tell of your heartache and how you survived it and moved on to other friendships. Part of this nurturing process is to show them that God is still in control and will help us work things out if we will only trust totally in him.

Ask your teens to share how they are feeling when something happens with a close friend. This will not only help you get them over this hurdle, but will also give them the courage and willingness to share their feelings with you on other important issues in the future.

NURTURING PUTS YOU AHEAD OF THE GAME

The hidden beauty of positively nurturing your teens when they need you is that one success builds on another, making them more and more open to your nurturing *and* teaching. Always, the key to nurturing is in listening, rather than finger pointing or preaching. Pray that they will truly believe you when you lovingly give your guidance. Trust in the God you serve to help bring your teen through any trouble that comes their way, and you will be miles ahead of 99 percent of parents of teens.

Most parents are good at teaching (preaching) and enjoy doing it. Nurturing, on the other hand, is foreign to many of us because so few of our parents modeled this patient, Christlike behavior. Learning the difference between teaching and nurturing, as well as mastering the art of each, will go a long way toward our ability to parent the way God wants us to. In the next chapter, we'll look at some classic mistakes parents make when they miss key opportunities for nurturing their kids.

Merely sticking with this book puts you in a select group of loving parents. If you have applied even half of the new ideas you've read so far, I'm sure your kids have seen a difference in your life and your love toward them. To talk about being like Jesus is totally different from trying our best to live and parent as he would have us do. Keep up the good work. You are giving Jesus something to smile about.

WHAT ABOUT YOU?

1. Here is a list of ideas that will help you reinforce your kids' faith in God. Add any additional thoughts of your own that can help you teach this most important area to your teens.

- Spend time in the Bible together.
- Pray together (in addition to mealtimes).
- Live out your daily quiet time as an example for them to see.
- Go to God with them for guidance, counsel, and strength.
- Read stories of heroes of the faith together.
- Purchase Christian books and music for them.
- Be open and honest about your trials and questions of your faith.
- Ask them for forgiveness when God prompts you to.

- Read Deuteronomy 6:7-9 together as a family. Ask how you can be a better teacher of the faith. Your kids and spouse have great ideas for you to use. Go to them often.

2. If your teens lose their love for God or start to backslide, what additional ways can you think of to lovingly nurture them back into a love for God?

- Pray for and with them.
- Ask them how you can best help.
- Don't let your words, actions, or judgment of them drive them away from God forever.
- Put your faith into practice and go as a family to feed the poor, help the homeless, visit those in the nursing homes, or be a friend to a teen in the juvenile home. Teens detest religious hypocrisy but deeply long for authenticity and putting one's faith into practice.
- Share how it's OK to be angry at God. God wants our open and honest friendship. He's strong enough to take the good with the bad. He merely wants us to trust him enough to listen carefully to his still, small voice as he speaks quietly to our hearts through his Word and other people. He will never stop loving us. As parents, our greatest challenge is to demonstrate this truth so our kids can get a glimpse of who God really is.
- Show the difference between Peter and Judas. Peter returned to God after weeping over his sin of deny-

ing Jesus three times and asked for forgiveness and another try. Judas gave up and never gave God a chance to prove his love for him or show his forgiveness.

- Simply be there with love and open arms for your prodigal child.

3. Consider each of the following issues that are vital for your teen's health and well-being. What are some ways you can teach about each one, and what are some ways you can nurture?

- Vehicle safety
- Eating disorders
- Importance of a good education and study habits
- Handling depression and thoughts of suicide
- Avoiding gang activities
- Respecting the law
- Being concerned about your community and world

4. Can you identify an area where you are inclined to tell, tell, tell, instead of nurture by listening and encouraging your teens to share their feelings?

5. Did your parents nurture you when you needed holding, listening to, or someone to simply understand how you felt? If not, why don't you think they were able to do this? Were your grandparents accustomed to hugging, sharing feelings, and encouraging kids to be heard as well as seen? What can you do to get your family started on the right track if this has not been a part of your heritage?

EXTRA POWER FOR PARENTS
FROM GOD'S WORD

Verses that teach:
On friendships: "Don't be fooled . . . bad company corrupts good character." (1 Corinthians 15:33)

On communication: "May the words of my mouth and the thoughts of my heart be pleasing to you, O Lord, my rock and my redeemer." (Psalm 19:14)

On husband-and-wife relationships: "You husbands must love your wives with the same love Christ showed the church. He gave up his life for her." (Ephesians 5:25)

On anger: "Dear friends, be quick to listen, slow to speak, and slow to get angry. Your anger can never make things right in God's sight." (James 1:19-20)

On sexual purity: "Give honor to marriage, and remain faithful to one another in marriage. God will surely judge people who are immoral and those who commit adultery." (Hebrews 13:4)

Verses on nurturing:
When you need God's strength: "I weep with grief; encourage me by your word." (Psalm 119:28)

When guilt chokes you: "I have swept away your sins like the morning mists. I have scattered your offenses like the clouds. Oh, return to me, for I have paid the price to set you free." (Isaiah 44:22)

When you feel all alone: "'For the mountains may depart and the hills disappear, but even then I will remain loyal to you. My covenant of blessing will never be broken,' says the Lord, who has mercy on you." (Isaiah 54:10)

"God has said, 'I will never fail you. I will never forsake you.' That is why we can say with confidence, 'The Lord is my helper, so I will not be afraid. What can mere mortals do to me?'" (Hebrews 13:5-6)

When God doesn't seem to be listening to our prayers: "Free those who are wrongly imprisoned and . . . stop oppressing those who work for you. Treat them fairly and give them what they earn. I want you to share your food with the hungry and to welcome poor wanderers into your homes. Give clothes to those who need them, and do not hide from relatives who need your help.

"If you do these things, your salvation will come like the dawn. Yes, your healing will come quickly. Your godliness will lead you forward, and the glory of the Lord will protect you from behind. Then when you call, the Lord will answer. 'Yes, I am here,' he will quickly reply." (Isaiah 58:6-9)

I hope these few verses show you that God has the ability to *teach* us and *nurture* us when we need him. If we search for him, he promises to be found. Learn the art of having God show you when the time is right to teach your kids and when you should minister to them in a loving, nurturing way. And never forget that when it comes to nurturing and teaching, there is a season for each!

CHAPTER 8

Classic Mistakes and the Walls They Build

"ABOUT A year and a half ago, [my parents] convinced me to go on this church retreat, and I went, and when I came back my entire room was emptied. No posters, magazines, books, newspapers, clock radio, stereo, music, CD player. Everything was gone. And they were going to pull me out of the school I was going to and put me in a Christian school. They were going to tell me that I couldn't see my boyfriend.

"That was because while I was away they had gone through and read all my things and stuff and found out that I wasn't the perfect little Christian princess that they had always thought I was. . . .

"I started to, like, freak out. There was just constant fighting, and constant—oh, my God, they just care so *much!*"[1]

This is seventeen-year-old Suzanne Jacobson, telling why she now lives with her boyfriend's family just down the road from her own parents.

An isolated incident? Hardly. Every day in America far too many parents and teens give up on each other. As hands fly upward in resignation, so also go the hopes, dreams, harmony, and joy of living as a happy, contented family.

Reacting with little or no communication or understanding is a classic mistake many of us make from time to time. My heart aches for these parents and their daughter. What a shame to act first and talk later. How tragic it must be to know that your actions have driven your daughter to live in the home of the very boy you tried so desperately to keep her from.

This short excerpt obviously doesn't tell all the story, especially not from the parents' point of view, but it does give us a glimpse of what can happen, and all too often does happen, when parents do things that drive a wedge between them and their teen. In this chapter we will discover classic mistakes and the walls they build. You'll find that most of the mistakes involve missing nurturing moments, failing to put our values to work and, instead, reacting out of our own emotions. We'll try to look at alternatives—how God would have us respond in love. In doing so, perhaps we can find some antidotes for this national epidemic.

HOW WALLS ARE BUILT

Before a wall can be built, the foundation must be set. We've spent our time together through this entire book discussing practical ways of building our homes and lives on the solid, rocklike foundation of God's words and ways. But even a wise builder can make a mistake by not referring to the blueprint and accidentally putting a wall where a door was supposed to be. In the next few pages let's learn from the mistakes of others so we don't put brick upon brick in the wrong places. We don't want to find out too late—as Suzanne Jacobson's parents did—that we've closed off the doorway to forgiveness and hope and re-placed it with walls of resentment and anger, pushing our child in the very direction we have prayed for them not to go.

CLASSIC MISTAKE #1: RESPECTING THINGS MORE THAN PEOPLE

Situation:
Your ten-year-old son wrestles with his friend in the living room, where wrestling is forbidden, and accidentally breaks an heirloom vase from your great-great-grandmother.

Respond or react?
This is an emotional moment, to say the least. Whatever happens in the moments that follow the splintering sound of glass will be a reminder for your son forever of (1) what is more important to you, him or the vase, and (2) how to respond when something terrible happens to a thing.

First of all, let me say that you do have the right to hold the vase in high esteem (though not as high as your son or any other person). It's OK to feel angry. After all, in addition to the vase, he did break the no-wrestling rule. But on the other hand, it wasn't very wise to have something that valuable out in the open. And please don't forget that it was an accident. If it was done on purpose, you would need to find out why and properly deal with that situation.

God's way.
What a great opportunity to show your son how important and valuable he is to you and God. Please realize that the vase is already smashed—you can't change that—so you might as well use this negative to your advantage by teaching a lesson that will last a lifetime. My sister Mary taught me to say something like, "I'm sorry this happened. I feel bad that you broke the rules, and I will miss my grandmother's vase very

much. Do you realize that your carelessness has caused me pain?"

After you have heard from him, teach him what God would do if he were there. "This is a great reminder to me that people are more important than things. Maybe I shouldn't have loved that vase so much. I do, however, love you a million times more than anything I will ever own. Let's never forget that all of our things were given to us by God, and I guess he didn't want me to hold on to that piece of ceramic quite so tightly."

If you can pray for the strength to respond like this, you will be gaining something priceless: your son's loyalty and love. He'll be more likely to come to you in the future if someone breaks his heart, all because you didn't drive him away by building a wall with your anger.

CLASSIC MISTAKE #2: GETTING ANGRY WHEN KIDS ACT THEIR AGE

Situation:
You've told your son a dozen times to wear his pads and helmet when roller blading. He forgets, wipes out, and breaks his arm.

Respond or react?
You run down the hill, raise your voice in anger, and blame him with a couple of "I told you so's" and a "why don't you ever listen," and of course you throw in "how can you be so stupid" because you're on a roll. He feels embarrassed, alone, and totally humiliated because all the neighbors are watching. By the time you calm down, realize his arm is in terrible shape, want to comfort him and take him to the hospital, you notice he pushes

away from you and is very distant. He stays that way for several weeks. Even when he does get over the neighborhood incident, things never seem quite the same again.

Reacting this way will do great damage. Since we are God in the flesh to our kids, they might very well feel that God also gets extremely upset when we make mistakes. Many teens don't want anything to do with their heavenly Father because all they have ever received from their earthly father and mother has been rejection and criticism.

God's way.

This is a classic time to lavish nurturing and love on your son. He knows he didn't follow the rules. Natural consequences taught that lesson. You don't even need to mention it.

It's your chance to teach a different lesson, one he will never forget, about the gentleness and compassion you express when you come to him responding as Jesus would.

God's way always builds friendships. Our natural way only builds walls.

CLASSIC MISTAKE #3: REFUSING TO SEE THINGS FROM THEIR POINT OF VIEW

Situation:

Your sixteen-year-old daughter gets dumped by a boy you care little for. She gets depressed and very despondent.

Respond or react?

Many parents use this tough time as an opportunity to put the boy down. They react with insensitivity because they are so relieved—not thinking about their daughter's crushed heart.

Seeing things from the viewpoint of your teen is very tough to do. You are much older and have forgotten (many times on purpose) what it was like to be her age. You must force yourself to try to feel as she does, with all of her insecurities and now the deep feelings of rejection. Parents who fail to step into their daughter's shoes and feel as she does often drive her to the next available pair of open arms. I've counseled with many teenage girls who have never recovered from the pain of rebounding from one bad situation to another.

God's way.

If she were Jesus' daughter, he would say, "I know how you feel. I've been dumped too. Even as I died for those I loved, they spit on me and hurled words that cut deeper than their nails or swords. But my Father waited with open loving arms for me. He loved me and hugged me and made everything all right again. Let me hold you and hurt with you and stay with you as long as it takes for you to replace your tears with feelings of hope."

CLASSIC MISTAKE #4: INSISTING YOUR RULES WILL MEET THEIR NEEDS

Situation:

You demand that your son stay away from the girl you disapprove of. You feel you know what's best for him. You know all you need to know about her reputation and family background. End of discussion.

Respond or react?

These types of "my way or the highway," "I have all the answers," and "I know what's best for you" decrees force your son to prove his manhood. He has needs that you are too busy to meet. Therefore, he is driven into her arms, life, and troubles. The truth is you do know what's best, but you don't know how to tactfully and lovingly convince him. Your need to be right has left a well of emptiness that he feels only she can fill. After all, he can't talk to you. You only have answers, not questions.

God's way.

I can almost hear God talking with your son beside a quiet riverbank or in a booth at McDonald's. "Do you remember what happened when you chose to put that paper clip in the wall socket? I told you you would get shocked, but you wanted to see for yourself. You are an extraordinary person. You will touch many lives for my glory in your lifetime. You are the hands-on type who needs to prove things for himself. Throw in your strong-willed, stubborn nature and you have the ingredients to be a powerful man of God someday. But for now you need to wake up, because you are about to make some big mistakes that will affect you for a long time to come. I love you more than you will ever know. You know that your parents disapprove of your dating Susan. Why are you fighting their wishes and best interest for your life? Look at how her past decisions have caused so much turmoil for her past boyfriends and their families. Your parents need you on their team if they are to guide you the way I want them to. What do you suggest be done to either get your parents to know her better or help her turn her life over to me so she will be forgiven of her past and not react as she has been because of it? You know as well as I do that without me in her life she is really on a dead-end road heading nowhere at breakneck speed."

If this were your conversation with your son, you would have met his greatest needs, which are to be respected and understood. You would have also put the ball in his court—as Jesus always did by answering questions with a question of his own. You see, Jesus' agenda was never to cram his view down people's throats but instead to get them to open their eyes and see the truth that his example illuminated.

Teenage love must be handled delicately at best, or the resulting walls can separate families for years to come.

CLASSIC MISTAKE #5: PUTTING DOWN YOUR TEEN IN PRIVATE AND PUBLIC

Situation:
Your thirteen-year-old daughter is at the awkward stage. She is unable to get along with anyone in the family, think before talking, or keep from crying over every little thing. Her body is freaking out on her, and she can't understand it or do anything about it. She is scared half to death.

Respond or react?
You react by letting off steam when talking to friends at church or relatives on the phone. At every chance, without realizing the damage you're doing, you tell people how tough it is being the parent of a new teen. You joke about her having PMS seven days a week.

When parents gossip in this way with little or no regard for their teen, they cause themselves more harm than they realize. Their daughter becomes even more confused, feeling betrayed and put down by the very people she needs encouragement from the most. When teens are in the eye of the storm, they need understanding—not comparisons to every other person who seems to have it all together.

God's way.

Remember what we discussed in chapter 6, situation #3, about your son being shy and awkward. Give him all the affirmation you can—both behind his back and to his face.

CLASSIC MISTAKE #6: TEACHING THAT "BIG BOYS DON'T CRY"

Situation:

Your mother dies. Your fifteen-year-old son takes the death of his favorite grandmother extremely hard because he was very close to her. He has never lost a loved one to death before and responds by ripping up the family picture album. He refuses to be consoled or talk to anyone, locking himself in his room for long stretches.

Respond or react?

Do you get him help, encourage him to cry, explain the grieving process to him, give him his space, let time help you out, and tell him you are here if and when he is ready or needs you? Or do you forbid him to cry and say as one fourteen-year-old girl wrote me: "My parents said that the funeral was over, and we were to get on with our lives. I was told not to live in the past and that tears were a sign of weakness. When I cried with you at our school, those were the first tears I shed in over four months since my grandmother died. Thank you for holding me and crying alongside of me. I felt like a little child, so weak and frail, but you respected me and never made me feel embarrassed. I can make it now."

Many of tomorrow's parents have never been taught how to cry, how to grieve and how healthy it is, how to work through pain step by step, how to trust in God as we ache and hurt, and how to see the big picture as God sees it. They have never learned that big boys who don't cry are seldom good at meeting anyone's needs, especially their own.

God's way.
Jesus cried when he heard of Lazarus's death. I think he was also crying about the people's lack of faith in him even after all his miracles and examples. Tears are God's cleansing agent for pain that nothing else can touch. Have your kids ever seen you cry over a world going to hell? Have you felt your children's pain to such an extent that you cried with them as you held them? The gift of tears melts away walls of pride and selfishness better than almost anything.

CLASSIC MISTAKE #7: IGNORING A PROBLEM, HOPING IT WILL DISAPPEAR

Situation:
You suspect that your daughter is forcing herself to vomit and lose weight. However, you can't handle one more problem with all the stress of being a single parent, so you ignore it and hope she'll grow out of it.

Respond or react?
While many parents condemn their daughters when the reality of bulimia or anorexia arrives on the scene, ignoring the problem can be deadly.

Your daughter is trying her best to become perfect so she will feel like she is special, lovable, and comparable to those she envies. If you ignore this problem, she will feel abandoned and unworthy of your precious time, effort, and energy in helping her through this living nightmare. The point of no return isn't very far down this bombed-out road built on a jagged cliff.

God's way.

When your daughter or one of her friends waves this flag that says "I'm hurting; please help me," jump to your feet and do all you can to get her the help she needs. God wants her to know how special she is—that she is a once-in-a-lifetime, priceless gift, given by him to your family and this world to show off his beauty and love. Convince her, no matter what or how long it takes, that she is wonderful just as she is and that you and God love her dearly. The world that has given her the unreachable goal of looking the way she thinks others want her to doesn't care for her or love her. Pray for her. Pray with her. Let your world revolve around her until she knows and truly believes that your words and wishes for her are from God himself.

CLASSIC MISTAKE #8: WINNING THE WAR—LOSING THE FRIENDSHIP

Situation:

Your daughter was told not to watch TV until all her homework was done. Of course, she has the TV on when you check on her. You ask if all her homework is done and she says, "No, but—" Without further discussion or hearing her through, you ground her and keep her from playing in the biggest soccer game of the year. She never gets to explain (even though it's not a valid excuse) that she merely didn't want to miss her favorite show and had only twenty minutes' worth of homework left.

Respond or react?

Reacting out of stored-up anger almost always causes parents to overreact and speak without thinking. This parent was having an ongoing battle over his daughter's not getting all A's as he did, and he couldn't imagine why or how she could take longer at homework than he did at her age. He has lost her friendship and respect. He caused her deep humiliation and heartache by not letting her be a hero during the big game—a loss she will never forget, and he may never live down.

God's way.

God would probably have walked in the door, sat down with her and enjoyed her company, then found out the homework situation. He might have responded, "My child, you are still acting your age. But you did do two hours of work before you stopped for a break. After that long I would have needed a breather, too. You have been showing maturity lately. I'm going to let you decide how and when to best get your work done. I realize you didn't follow the law to the letter, but what's most important here is that we respect each other and that you get plenty of rest tonight so you can win the big game tomorrow."

God's worth as a parent would never be wrapped up in how perfect his kids were or whether they obeyed his every word and thought. I think an overriding friendship and love for others would let him do what Steve Winwood's song suggests, "Roll with It, Baby!"

WHAT ABOUT YOU?

1. What walls have you built between yourself and your teen that need to be torn down once and for all? Whom can you count on for godly counsel in discussing this area of need with you? Are you willing to ask for forgiveness in areas where you've failed? God is ready to give you the strength and wisdom to do what is needed to rebuild a stronger bond between you and your teen. Please let him help you, starting now.

2. What *things* have you allowed to become more important than your child or spouse? Has this chapter helped you realize that things will perish but your child will live forever? Do any of your toys or hobbies own you? Once they start taking time away from your family or God, it's time to carefully evaluate who owns whom.

3. Do you have habits that send messages to your child that might be building walls between you? For example, by continually telling your teen how disappointed you are in his grades you are keeping him from growing close to you.

4. Do you play favorites with your children without realizing it? All of us do it to some degree from time to time. Part of this is normal, but if it starts to get out of hand and one child perceives that you consistently favor another, it can build walls that are very difficult even to perceive, let alone talk about. It's very healthy from time to time to sit down at a family meeting and ask where you have goofed up and what you can do to better meet your children's needs.

5. God is the great bridge builder and wall buster. Go to him now and ask for forgiveness for the mistakes you have made in parent-

ing. You are not alone. This chapter greatly convicted me as I wrote it, and it drove me to my knees many times. Every parent has regrets. No parent before us or after us is or ever will be perfect. Ask God for the strength and wisdom to make tomorrow better than today, and be wise enough to leave your confessed mistakes in his hands. If you are in a group of parents, why not stand in a circle holding hands and give all of your past mistakes to your heavenly Father once and for all.

EXTRA POWER FOR PARENTS
FROM GOD'S WORD

> Most important of all, continue to show deep love for each other, for love covers a multitude of sins. (1 Peter 4:8)

Every one of the eight examples in this chapter could have been handled as Jesus would have, if only love were the motive, rather than self-interest. Love must be lived out most when we feel like it the least. Our teens need it most when they seem to deserve it least. Love is a wall destroyer and a bridge builder, because love is personified in God himself. Let God's love and nature work for you and your child today.

> Remember that the temptations that come into your life are no different from what others experience. And God is faithful. He will keep the temptation from becoming so strong that you can't stand up against it. When you are tempted, he will show you a way out so that you will not give in to it. (1 Corinthians 10:13)

God always has solutions for our problems! Every single one! Even those dealing with our teens! Every parenting problem you will ever face has already been dealt with by countless other parents over the centuries. Any problem that will ever come between you and your teen, please understand that God has allowed it. Just as when he asked Peter to walk on water, he wants you to trust him through any problem you ever face. You don't need to act out of your anger or ignorance. Turn to God, and together you can build a bridge between you and your child and tear down all remaining walls.

God loves to prove his power to and through us. God won't allow problems to enter our home that he can't help us handle any more than we would put candy in front of a five-year-old and tell the child not to eat it. Walk by faith, not by sight.

> Get rid of all bitterness, rage, anger, harsh words, and slander, as well as all types of malicious behavior. Instead, be kind to each other, tenderhearted, forgiving one another, just as God through Christ has forgiven you. (Ephesians 4:31-32)

God's kingdom has no room for reacting out of malice and continually getting even or remembering wrongs done to you. God commands us to get rid of this damaging stuff that ruins homes and severs relationships. The answer is given at the end of the verse: Forgive your teen as God has forgiven you!

> Humble yourselves under the mighty power of God, and in his good time he will honor you. Give all your worries

and cares to God, for he cares about what happens to you.
(1 Peter 5:6-7)

I love the picture this verse portrays. God's mighty power is over us, protecting us from life's storms. If we will only recognize his presence in our lives, being humble will come automatically. Pride can't exist when we know God is in our room. And just as he died for all our sins, he is also willing to take on all our worries and cares. Read it again. Isn't it wonderful? He wants all our anxieties! Praise God!

Yet true religion with contentment is great wealth.
(1 Timothy 6:6)

God wants us to be contented and full of peace and joy as we think about our family—in this house, driving this car, with our current job, with the same hips, neighbors, and clothes. We are rich if we have children. (Ask anyone who has ever lost a child.) Be at peace with yourself, God, and your children. Enjoy them. Watch them at night while they sleep and marvel at God's peaceful miracle. Let your life be a great big "thank you" back to God for all he has done for you. Start right now. Go hug your kids.

Notes
1. E. Jean Carroll, "Womanhood Has a Nose Ring, an Attitude, and Some Questions for a Dying Culture," *Esquire*, February 1994, p. 59.

CHAPTER 9

Don't Douse Their Desire

MICHAEL JORDAN shocked the sporting world when he retired from basketball to give Major League Baseball a try. All eyes were on him. Wherever he played, the ball parks were sold out. Many bet against him, many for him, but every sports fan in America was keeping an eye on Michael's daily progress.

The headlines continually asked, "Can Michael hit a curve ball?" In the midst of this daring new venture, Michael said something that is at the core of his sports success: "I'm not afraid to fail, but I refuse not to try!"

I wrote that statement down and started sharing it with my school assembly programs. Young people caught onto it. They liked the sound of it, and many told me they had never been challenged with anything like it before. Oh, if only our children would believe this statement, internalize it, and dare to live it out for the glory of God, they would be difference makers that the world would not soon forget.

"I'm not afraid to fail, but I refuse not to try!" That was the apostle Peter's way of life. He may have put his foot in his mouth more than the other disciples, but just as when he stepped out onto the water during the storm, usually his foot was the only one moving.

Paul took on the uttermost parts of the world with this way of thinking. He refused not to try, not to share, not to go a step further, not to be full of joy and hope, even in prison.

I want to look very closely at the ingredients that will help our teens become confident enough to try new things and be wise risk takers—not foolishly jumping off cliffs to be recognized and applauded by their peers, but taking the risk of sharing their faith or bowing their head before a meal, all for the applause of heaven.

Let's discover what it will take for our kids to dare to touch their world with the love and message of the most unpolitically correct character in the universe: Jesus Christ. We'll also find out in this chapter what stifles confidence, creativity, and newness. Let's help our kids develop an attitude that looks at the world with love, excitement, and positive expectancy.

THE RIGHT KIND OF FAILURE VS. THE WRONG KIND OF SUCCESS

To me, the right kind of failure is the Thomas Edison type. When asked about failing at ten thousand different experiments to find the perfect filament for the incandescent light, he replied, "Oh, no, we haven't failed. We've found ten thousand ways that won't work."

The right kind of failure is Billy Graham trying to lead every single lost person in the stadium to a saving, loving relationship with Jesus Christ. They don't all come, but many do—and Billy never stops trying.

The right kind of failure is any high jumper putting the bar up one more notch to try to better his best. He would rather try a new height, knowing he might fall flat on his face and be laughed at, than settle with prestige in the midst of mediocrity.

On the other hand, the wrong kind of success can be very damaging. Young people and their parents who settle for this cheap substitute for achievement are setting themselves up for a sad disappointment somewhere down the road.

The person who is a perfectionist and is unwilling to ever be wrong will never grow or change and forever feels trapped. Many parents demand perfection with such intensity that they frighten their child into the comfort zone of only trying to do what they know they can do perfectly. Those are the kids who never make eye contact and don't know how to start or carry on a conversation. They are emotional and social cripples who stand little chance at succeeding at life.

The wrong kind of success comes as a result of cheating, taking advantage of others, always wondering what you can gain from people instead of asking God what they need and how you could serve them.

The rich young man turned his back on Jesus and refused to follow him because of his vast wealth. His so-called success led him toward a life without Jesus and an eternity in hell. He definitely missed the mark.

What can I do, as the coach and referee of my kids, to make sure I don't accidentally guide them toward being self-seeking persons who only have their own interest and comfort at heart? How can I encourage and help build their desire to try new things, live out what they know to do, be a leader and not a follower—instead of stifling their potential by pouring the waters of fear and discouragement on the small, burning embers that I've spent their lifetime trying to kindle?

Let's get a glimpse of five ideas to help fan the flames of our children's potential and, at the same time, keep us from dousing their desire.

KINDLING TIP #1: AVOID "I TOLD YOU SO"

When parents throw a fault or mistake back in their teens' face, it absolutely stops them cold and pushes them back further into the cave of fear. If you want to know how to be certain that your kids will be paralyzed the next time they have the opportunity to meet someone new, just keep reminding them of their past mistakes. It's called self-fulfilling prophecy, and once you (their number-one hero and supposedly their number-one encourager) convince them that they are losers, it's extremely difficult to reverse the trend.

KINDLING TIP #2: DON'T PREACH

How do you like it when someone gets in your face and preaches at you? Always telling, never asking. Acting like a pillar of perfection, instead of someone who has failed often but keeps reaching for God's hand. A finger pointer! You feel just like your child and me and everyone else on the face of this planet: angry and resentful and totally turned off!

As we discussed in chapter 7, many times our kids need nurturing—not preaching. And unfortunately, those are usually the times we're raring to get up on our soapbox and let 'em have it. Remember what we've talked about: Recognize the opportunity to put your values into practice. Ask yourself how Jesus would respond. Then give your kids all the love, affirmation, and nurturing you can.

KINDLING TIP #3: NEVER DISCOURAGE TRYING AND EFFORT

A lesson from my school staff-development seminar entitled "Are We Teaching or Touching Lives?" fits nicely here.

When the class is asked a question, what answer is the easiest to give? Most say, "I don't know"—but it's not the easiest because it has implications of "I haven't studied," "I don't know this material," "I'm not prepared," and of course "I'm not smart enough to know this answer." The easiest answer, no matter what the question, is always the right answer—when you know for sure that it is indeed the right answer. When a teacher asks, "What is the capital of Michigan?" the easiest answer will come from those students who know that Lansing is the capital. They give the right answer but grow very little. They stay totally within their comfort zone.

On the other hand, a student who thinks the answer is Dallas and raises a hand to give it a try has taken the biggest risk and put forth the most effort. We both know that if he is laughed at, he probably won't answer any more questions the rest of the year. His teacher would have failed him miserably if she didn't come to his aid when he was being laughed at or make special effort in applauding his risk-taking ability at trying for the correct answer.

It's the same in our homes. I've always heard that you shouldn't cry over spilled milk, but I never knew why until recently. It's because our homes are places where practice should be encouraged, not where perfection should be demanded. Home is the one safe place where we should be free to ask questions, learn to talk things out, spill our milk, and clean it up.

KINDLING TIP #4: TEACH GOOD SOCIAL SKILLS

Many of today's teenagers have very poor social skills. A firm handshake is as foreign as speaking another language to many of them. We must model for our teens how to treat people with respect, use common courtesies, and communicate clearly, or they'll spend much of their lives with their social foot in their mouth. You are the buffer zone between your awkward teen and the future social situations awaiting them.

Show your children how to interact with others in your home and church. By watching parents enjoy themselves without alcohol or other drugs, our kids can get a look at what most young people never see—people having fun, drug-free. Take your teens out to dinner at a fancy restaurant. Have them cook a meal for you and serve it with all the trimmings. Social skills are definitely one of those areas where experience is the best teacher. Please remember that spilled milk is the very thing we aren't supposed to cry about. Our homes are places for practice, not perfection.

Each day should give our children chances to interact with other people. Let them call for the movie times or the menu prices. Have them give the Christmas gift to the paperboy, thanking him for doing such a good job. Encourage your children of all ages to make good eye contact, speak loudly enough to be heard, give firm handshakes, continue looking at the person speaking until he or she is finished. One of the reasons so many teens dress and act the way they do is simply that they have no other ways in which to gain attention.

People are more important than things. Give the gift of respecting people and using things instead of the other way around. Don't just talk about being against racism; truly pray for strength to love all people as if they were Jesus himself. There is too much hatred and anger being modeled in this world of ours. Let your teens grow into adulthood remembering their parents as warm, loving people who treated strangers merely as friends not yet made. And above all else, don't forget to enjoy your kids when you are in social settings. Nervous and perfectionistic parents raise very neurotic kids. Give your kids a break when it comes to acting their age, but most of all, give them enjoyable opportunities to learn to love people.

KINDLING TIP #5: DON'T ISOLATE YOUR KIDS FROM REALITY

Many parents try to protect their kids from the world and its dangers. Isolating your kids isn't protection; it merely prolongs the learning process. What a shame it must be never to practice throughout your childhood how to rely on God, thus not knowing how to follow his direction as an adult. Natural consequences are God's way of smoothing out the rough edges during the learning and growing process.

Teach your kids how to decide whether a certain TV show is good or harmful. Do the same with movies, music, friends, and so on. Then give them opportunities to be around others so they can get some "playing time" in life's game. They will fall short in the big game if we keep them away from all the tough, demanding practices and scrimmages.

SEVENTH GRADE AT MY HOUSE

While I was writing this chapter, God gave me a chance to live out some more of my own advice. My thirteen-year-old daughter, Emily, was extremely discouraged and had failed to hand in several assignments in one of her classes. The teacher contacted us and told us that these papers had to be turned in or she would fail. I'd talked briefly with Emily, telling her that this wasn't the end of the world but it was something that she had to see through so she could learn to trust God when bigger challenges come her way.

I drove her back to school late that afternoon (knowing that she would have died with embarrassment if I had showed up during school hours). We went through her locker, which made her room look clean, and retrieved what we thought were all of her unfinished papers. Just as we were leaving, her teacher walked out of his room, leaving for the day. Emily was a bit nervous about talking with him, so I thought this would be a good time to show her that teachers were normal human beings that could be talked to like anyone else. He was impressed that we had come the very day of his call, and after looking through his file, he found two additional assignments she had lost.

Emily was so relieved at her teacher's kindness and understanding that she went straight to her room after we got home and finished half of her work in three straight hours. In two more days she was totally caught up. That evening after school we sat down and talked. Because I had gently seized the opportunity to help her through this stressful time, I had earned the right to share some lessons with her that I hope will be etched on her mind forever:

- This family sticks together and deeply cares about one another.
- She has what it takes to get and stay organized, get

caught up if she falls behind, and talk to her teacher to discuss problems or ask questions.

- Being organized will help every area of her life.
- God will give her the strength to do what is best for her throughout her life.
- She can always come to Mom or Dad and tell us when she is troubled or needs advice.

We grew a bit closer that night because I let her save face instead of further humiliating her by slapping on a punishment. She is just entering the turbulent teens and needs all the help my wife and I can give her.

HIS WAY OF GETTING EVEN

As we've learned, helping children find successes, however small, is a great way to nudge them even closer to a life full of feeling capable and special. However, a seventeen-year-old boy with leadership abilities written all over his face recently showed me the other side of this priceless coin called "desire."

He had just been kicked out of school. He had the weight of the world on his shoulders, resented his well-to-do parents, and was into drugs and sleeping with every girl in sight. He had heard my talk, and afterward we hit it off. Because I was about to leave town and wouldn't see him again, he gave me the lowdown on why he was deliberately ruining his life:

"My parents have never once praised me like you described doing with your kids. They have always made it their duty to remind me of everything I've ever done wrong.

"I can't tell you the last time my dad sat down with me and

talked like we are doing right now. They always seem to talk down to me like I'm a stranger or something. We used to be friends when I was real little. I just want so much to be a family again.

"I never felt like I could live up to their standards. But they've put me down for the last time! I hated being humiliated in front of others when they would always compare me to others. So I finally left home. I simply gave in. I figured, you win! I'm a failure! Why should I try anymore?"

Talking with him broke my heart and gave me renewed purpose for my work with teens and parents—and mostly my own family. When I got home I hugged my children and told them how priceless they are to me and to God. Yours are waiting. Tell them the same thing.

WHAT ABOUT YOU?

1. Why not write Michael Jordan's statement on a three-by-five card and give each family member a copy to carry around in their pocket for one week? At dinnertime you could each discuss how you put it into practice each day. *"I am not afraid of failure, but I refuse not to try."*

2. Can you identify ways in which you have crushed your children's creativity or belief in their own ability to achieve great things? Have you:

- Pushed your perfectionism on them?
- Demanded that they live up to your success?
- Deliberately made fun of them for making a mistake?

142

- Laughed at them when they tried something new and looked awkward doing it?
- Gotten angry when they tried something new and failed?
- Called them a derogatory name and failed to ask for their forgiveness?

If you need to, why not ask for forgiveness and your kids' help in how you can better meet their needs and help them dare to be different. Let them know that you are in their corner. Tell them, show them, and live out your love for them.

3. In what areas of your teen's life can you give more encouragement? What skills does your teen need to gain more confidence in? Whom could you and your teen talk to, to find out how they achieved success in a certain area that seems to be troubling your son or daughter?

4. Is there an area where you find yourself "preaching" at your child in a condescending manner? If so, why not turn that area totally over to God? He is more than capable in his ability to guide your child over the rough tracks of life. Show your faith in God by "letting go and letting God." Your teen will see your faith in action and appreciate being treated as an adult.

EXTRA POWER FOR PARENTS FROM GOD'S WORD

What this means is that those who become Christians become new persons. They are not the same anymore, for the old life is gone. A new life has begun! (2 Corinthians 5:17)

You are a child of God. You *can* change in any area where you have battles, because God is bigger and stronger than any trial that will ever come your way. You can now be the visionary of your child's needs. You have the hope that your son or daughter needs to be their best for God. Claim and memorize this verse. It's power just waiting to be lived out. Let God show you your "life-touching" skills. Let him shine through you today!

For God is working in you, giving you the desire to obey him and the power to do what pleases him. (Philippians 2:13)

What exciting news! We don't have to handle life on our own. God is our great enabler. He is our strength and our backbone. He wants to show the world how wonderful and confident we are to live like him. Please give God the chance to work in you and have your life represent his will on earth.

And you will know the truth, and the truth will set you free. (John 8:32)

When our children know the truth, they are free to let God show himself in their lives. All children have the right to know the following things:

- You, as their parent, aren't perfect.
- You also need God to make it through the day.

- You need your kids just as much as they need you.
- We have failed but kept on, and so can they.
- Failing at something or being laughed at for trying are part of life, so don't miss out because of fear.
- You've pushed them too hard at times or were too pre-occupied with your own worries and didn't spend enough time with them.
- You want to be close friends with them and be a part of their good and bad times.

No, dear friends, I am still not all I should be, but I am focusing all my energies on this one thing: Forgetting the past and looking forward to what lies ahead, I strain to reach the end of the race and receive the prize for which God, through Christ Jesus, is calling us up to heaven. (Philippians 3:13-14)

Forget past failures. They are only part of the learning process. Keep looking out your windshield and get rid of your rearview mirror. Don't let Satan convince you that with failure, discouragement automatically follows. Refuse to take your eyes off Jesus!

Conclusion

COLLEGE REGISTRATION—the highlight of every young adult's life. (Tell your children that college is a breeze. That is, *if* you can get through registration!)

There I was. A high school graduate in the fall of 1969. Afraid of crowds and wishing to be anywhere in the universe but here. And the only way I was going to get my classes was to elbow my way through angry mobs of smart, good-looking kids who all seemed to know precisely what they were doing. After waiting in lines for over three hours, I was greeted with sign after sign that told me how much I was loved and wanted: SECTION CLOSED! CLASS FULL! Five classes in a row. All I had was one skimpy credit hour.

My best friend, Steve McKinley, who had enough confidence for both of us, had just taken his fifteen credit hours and left for home. There I was, left standing on my own to fend for myself. How could a real friend just leave me here to handle these selfish cutthroats?

I made my first college decision. Totally on my own I said, "I'm quitting!" One quick glance around. No one cares for me. I'm out of here. I spotted the door and was heading directly for it. Avoiding all eye contact, feeling like a whipped pup too scared to stand up to the neighbor's cat, I wanted to cry and hide and never be seen again in public. I felt like I was three years old, alone in the dark, and I wanted my mom.

As I was making my way sheepishly toward the door, I felt an arm around my shoulder. Without looking up, I heard a caring voice ask, "What are you doing?"

Continuing toward the door I said, "Quitting."

"Quitting what?" he asked.

"College. I'm quitting college."

With a chuckle, trying his best to offer me some hope, he said, "This isn't college; it's registration."

"Then I'm quitting registration!"

This kind man invited me to his counseling office, helped me get the classes I had waited in so many lines for earlier, and proceeded to change the course of my life forever.

First, he made me laugh. He asked, "What *is* your problem?"

Feeling sorry for myself, I said, "I've been out there for over three hours and all I get is SECTION CLOSED, CLASS FULL. My buddy has his classes, and I'm here all alone and don't know what to do."

He then brought humor to the scene to take my mind off my troubles. He said, "I know! I've been watching you for over an hour and in all my years of education, you were *the* most pitiful thing I've ever seen!"

We both laughed, and I realized that what my grandma had loved to say was true once again: "This too shall pass."

Next, he took care of me. He knew what was wrong. He knew it even before I told him. With a very pleasant smile, the kind you get when you have the perfect solution to someone's problem, he said, "Write the classes you need on this add slip, and you can get them in room so-and-so."

I couldn't believe it. How could anything be so simple when I had just suffered for over three hours! I felt like Calvin from "Calvin and Hobbes." "Just like that? It's that easy? That's all there is to it?" I must admit that piece of paper called an "add slip" still holds fond memories in my heart.

He then said four words that I had never heard in all my years of formal education. "I need you here." He looked directly into my eyes, and as hard as I tried not to believe that I could be needed, somehow I knew he meant every word. *I need you here.* How could four simple words give so much hope?

I responded, "What do you mean, you need *me* here? I was about to quit a few minutes ago."

With every ounce of persuasion he had, he started in. "I need you here. I need you to help me look for students who are scared and ready to give up, like you just were. You have something called *empathy.* You know what it feels like to drown because you were on your way down.

"Do you know how many students head out that door before I can get to them? Do you have any idea how many young people will never enter those doors because they've grown up believing they aren't college material? You are going to be a life-toucher. You'll get your sheepskin like everyone else here, but in the meantime you and I are going to be on the lookout for pain and hopelessness. I need you here because you are going to help me turn lives around."

He had no way of knowing that he was helping me choose my fork in the road. Today those words are the focal point of every speech I give, every book I write, and every letter I answer.

Talk about a life-changing, teachable, reachable moment! Because of Chuck Holland's wisdom in transforming a disaster into a moment of hope, my life took on new meaning. I didn't need my buddy to make it through the day. I even stopped looking for my mom (until I got hungry, that is!).

One remarkable thing about having your life altered forever is that you hardly realize it at the time. I had no way of knowing as I sat scared and confused in that counseling office that I would become a public speaker and writer. And you have no idea what your life-touching skill will produce in your children or the people you encounter daily. We must be on the lookout for teachable opportunities, moment by moment. We must seize the moments when they are handed to us, gift wrapped and ready to go.

Ask yourself, Who needs an uplifting word from me today? Who hasn't had an arm around their shoulders in months? Who has been absent from church for several weeks or months with no phone call, no letter? no one to say, "I need you here"? no one to declare, "You are special to God and to me. It just isn't the same around here without you"? The cure for pain is often simple, and we hold it in the palm of our hands just as Chuck Holland held that add slip. But we fail to notice people struggling and often simply don't take the time to be a life-toucher.

Be one today. Someone is waiting—probably walking the other way—shoulders drooped, no eye contact, heading for the door. Quite often they are our children. Help them hang in there and achieve their marvelous, incredible potential. Tell them they look pitiful and make them laugh—before it's too late.

Values Reinforcers

IF I COULD wave a magic wand over the environment surrounding your teen, I would make the following fifteen assets a consistent reality in their world. I call these "values reinforcers" because without them, our values evaporate in a confusing and compromising world. Rarely do I find young people who have all of these assets in need of counsel. Sit down with your kids and discuss these assets with them. Ask for their opinion on what changes can be made to make these a permanent part of your home. This will help give your children ownership as well as a feeling of importance and capability. See how many you are providing for your family now, and work on the ones that seem to be weak at this time.

1. A family that supports and protects one another.
Gangs are never needed when a young person feels support and appreciation at home. An environment that is safe and happy breeds a sense of importance and belonging. Teens who don't feel connected to something greater than themselves will search the world over to find a way to prove their worth. Kids coming from strong homes have no need to prove their significance by having premarital sex or using drugs. They know what real,

unselfish love, with no strings attached, is all about because they have seen it lived out in their home. Therefore when the counterfeit comes along, they will spot it in an instant. Make sure that your house is a warm, loving home where your child can find a safe haven from a very demanding and coldhearted world.

2. A strong bond of friendship between parent and teen.

It's been said that teens will go to people they respect when they need someone to talk to. I believe, however, that if a strong relationship doesn't already exist, there is no way they will approach that person. Teens have told me over the years that they would love to go to their parents with their questions and to look to them as a resource for help and advice—but they are afraid of how their parents might react. No one wants to share fears and weak areas with someone who seems to be too busy or insensitive to care. Treat your kids as your friends. Have fun with them and share your thoughts and heart, and you'll be opening the door for them to do the same.

3. Parents with whom teens can talk about anything.

Without the friendship and bond we just spoke of, open communication will never take place. Very few teens feel they can talk to their parents about serious and intimate issues such as sex, their feelings of inadequacy, peer pressure to drink and use drugs, and tough questions like "If God really cares why doesn't he answer my prayers?" Help your teen be one of the fortunate young people in this country who can go to their parents with any and every concern they have. Give them the edge they need to develop and grow, with the assurance that their questions are being answered by someone who loves them as much as life itself. If you or I need someone to talk with but have no one to turn to, we feel pretty bad, don't we? For a teen this seems like the end of the world! Be there for them. Ask them to help you learn how to talk to them. You will be pleasantly surprised at their interest in meeting you halfway.

4. Parents who are actively involved in their teen's school, church, sports, and other outside activities.

Parents who get to know their teen's teachers, coach, youth pastor, and friends' parents almost guarantee successful teen years. It takes time and effort, but the good news is that if we spend time with them now, they will want to spend time with us later. It's like the song "Cat's in the Cradle" by Harry Chapin. If we are too busy pursuing life to spend time getting to know our kids, they will have no reason to please us by their wise choices. A young boy in a juvenile home told a youth worker, "My parents weren't involved in my life when I obeyed all the rules. They didn't even know I existed. Now I have them all to myself for two solid hours every Wednesday and Saturday during visitation." What a shame that tragedies have to happen before some parents desire to throw their arms and lives around their kids.

5. Authentic parents.

If your standards for yourself are as high as they are for your children, you will never be guilty of not walking your talk or living out your faith.

Many parents want their kids to live like saints but refuse to follow the same rules. One troubled teen told me, "My parents tell me not to drink, but they can't get through one night without booze. They yell at me and my friends about drinking and driving, but my dad has taken many baby-sitters home after he's been drinking all night. Now that they got divorced, my mom has her boyfriend stay at our house overnight. She better not try and preach to me about morals." That boy had so much anger and bitterness built up in him that it's just a matter of time before he begins acting on it. Be parents worth following because you are sticking to the same ideals you would have liked your parents to live by.

6. Positive discipline.
Discipline is synonymous with training, not punishment. Positive discipline comes from parents who try to coach their kids rather than drill them and demand perfection. Let your teens know what you *expect.* Then make sure and *inspect* whatever they have done, whether it be cleaning the car or finding out who chaperoned the party they were at Friday night.

Think of all the things our kids do right. Now think of all the things we so easily catch them doing wrong. Just like missing two questions out of a hundred, they probably do ninety-eight things right for each two things they do wrong. A wise parent recently told me that we don't have the right to catch our kids doing the two wrong things if we have failed to catch them doing any of the ninety-eight right things.

To respect God means that we know he loves us enough to show us the right way to do something if we are doing it wrong. Positive discipline will help our kids respect us in that same way.

7. Parents who know what's going on.
No one will check up on your child like you will. If you don't put forth the effort to know what's going on in your child's emotional, physical, social, and spiritual life, you can be assured that no one else will either. Parents need to link up with

one another to organize a network that will work together to monitor teens' activities during the week and especially on the weekends. Obviously there is no way to know everything your teen does—nor would we want to. (Boy, you can say that again!)

I'm not talking about being a drill sergeant. But I see far too many parents who are strangers to their teens and their peers. In a few short years they will be on their own, and no one will be checking up on their whereabouts or activities. The world awaiting them is cold and indifferent. Show them you care by doing your best to guide them in and out of wise choices, activities, and friendships. Stay involved.

8. Enjoyable time at home.

Well-adjusted young people who can look others in the eye, as well as have a sparkle in their own, almost always come from a home with a pleasant atmosphere. Ask yourself: When was the last time I laughed out loud with my kids? Isn't it easy to get caught up in the stress that life throws at us and find that you haven't laughed in several days or weeks? I try so hard to make our home a happy place. Often I catch myself demanding perfection from my kids to a point that I'm no more than an old grouch. All of us learn from my wife, Holly, about laughing easily and often. I'm convinced that laughter—like joy and inner peace—come from knowing that you aren't trying to hide anything from God.

Do your kids enjoy being alone? It's very healthy for them to enjoy their own company as well as relax and think or listen to music. (I realize that much of their music is a direct contradiction to the words *relax* and *think,* but then again, so was most of ours.

Of course, damaging and destructive lyrics are something that must be dealt with. Be gentle and positive, but do address that issue because those lyrics are programming your teen toward self-destruction.)

Do you as a family enjoy each other's company? Are the phrases "I love you" and "I love you, too" heard often enough around your home? Are put-downs prohibited? Do you encourage each other to make up before bedtime to avoid sleeping on your anger? All in all, your home should be an oasis where any of you can become refreshed after a day in the scorching world.

9. Positive adult role models.
I am very fortunate to have many friends who take an active interest in my children. Several of my friends have taken my kids out for a meal at different times, at my request, just to talk with them about a difficult time they might be going through. It's extremely important that our kids hear the same consistent messages from other adults that they hear from us.

In thinking through all of the adults in your child's world (coach, youth pastor, teacher, neighbor, your friends, Scout leader, etc.), how many of them help your child desire a more godly life? Our kids need all the help we can give them, and few things undermine what we are trying to pass on to them like adults who send mixed messages. Be willing to gently confront any adults who might be harmful to your kids. Just as you protected your kids when they were little by making sure their baby-sitters were responsible and capable, you need to pay attention to their environment even when they're teens.

10. *A safe and encouraging school climate.*

In America over one hundred thousand guns are taken to schools every day. If your children's school isn't safe, please get them into another school.

I realize that everyone isn't able to send their kids to a Christian school. I can't encourage you enough, however, to pray about what you could give up to make it financially possible for your kids to learn in an environment that backs up your family values. My three kids have been in a Christian school for only two years, and it has proven to be the single greatest thing we have done for them next to encouraging them to accept Christ as their personal Savior.

At a recent graduation in my old high school, a board member told the graduating class that they should feel secure in the fact that for twelve years the school system has protected them from the "censored Christian Right." I turned to Holly and said, "They actually feel that their job is to protect my kids from my beliefs."

Become actively involved in your school. Get to know the teachers as well as the curriculum. Our kids' minds and their views of right and wrong are at stake. Please forgive me if I am causing any pain or guilt over this intense subject. I have seen so many lives that have been deeply affected because parents failed to investigate the environment their child was caught in.

11. *Positive peers with similar beliefs.*

There isn't much I can say about this subject that you don't already know. If your teen seems to be attracted to a peer with a negative influence, one of two things is probably the cause: Either your teen's self-image matches that of the friend, or the friend is providing the feeling of being needed and loved that your teen isn't finding at home.

Here are several tips that hundreds of successful parents whom I've had the pleasure of meeting over the past twenty years have shared with me:

Model friendships with people who have healthy attitudes and habits. If your kids can see you enjoying life with friends who don't use alcohol or profanity, they will get the idea that healthy, positive friends can be fun for them as well. Many teens never get the opportunity to observe healthy relationships. Give them this precious gift.

Get to know your child's friends. Negative peers with their own agendas seldom allow themselves to get very close to authority figures who might expose them. I counsel many troubled parents each year who tell me they wish they had invaded their teen's world in a positive, loving way. When your teen's friends get used to looking you in the eye and talking with you face-to-face, they will usually think twice about talking your teen into doing something that they know would get them into hot water with you.

Spend time with the families of your teen's friends. Parents who get to know the entire family of their teen's friend are giving themselves an ace in the hole. Yes, this takes a tremendous amount of time—but so does picking up broken pieces and damaged lives. Have the family over to your home, and show how enjoyable it can be playing games and having laughs without using alcohol or drugs. This family may be a mission field for your family. Wise Christian parents never cast off a teen's troubled friend until they have taken the time and effort to pray and do their best to touch his or her life with the love of Jesus.

Make a written list of positive characteristics of healthy, well-intentioned friends. Together with your teen, write down qualities of healthy and unhealthy friends. When someone comes into your teen's life about whom you have serious questions, simply have your child go over the list of qualities and objectively evaluate this person's character. Your teen helped come up with the list, so all you are doing is putting the ball back in your teen's court.

Pray with your teen that God will bring his chosen friends into your teen's life. Whenever I meet Christian teens who are attracted to friends with strong values, prayer almost always has played a huge part in it. Many teens have told me that they grew up hearing their parents pray for their future friends as well as their husband or wife. Praying for God's protection and wisdom in making the right choices about friends helps your child recognize that God wants to take an active part in our everyday lives. God is just as thrilled when our kids go to him for advice as we are when they come to us. You will never stand taller in your children's eyes than when you stoop down to pray with them.

12. Positive media input.

Here are two statements I hope you never forget:

1. This is the first generation to be totally immersed in the media while growing up.

2. If you allow your children to watch and listen to whatever they choose whenever they wish, you are wasting your time taking them to church or teaching them your values.

Many teens have never been told that the media—and the superstars getting rich off of it—do not have our best interests at heart. The junk that is pumped into our kids' minds and hearts for an average of two to four hours each day needs a filtering system to protect kids from the full force of its poison. *You are that filter.* You must be willing to model wise media use yourself and have the courage and fortitude to make tough decisions about which media input upholds your family values. If you leave your children to their own discretion and desires, you might as well admit that our culture is raising your children.

Kids of all ages feel safe when standards are set and upheld. I'm not talking about being a control freak. Parents who try to control every ounce of their child's life end up handing the world an emotional cripple. I am, however, trying to make as strong a statement as I can that if you let the secular media enter your children's world at the average rate, you will end up with some serious challenges in imparting your values to them. Help your kids learn to discern for themselves what programming will make them more like Jesus and what programming they would feel ashamed of if he were sitting next to them watching and listening.

13. Positive involvement in after-school activities.

Let's face it; if your kids aren't involved in after-school activities such as sports, music, church, or Scouting, they have lots of time on their hands to get into trouble. Like all of us, kids need direction and structure.

Many parents regret not encouraging their children to expand their areas of interest by getting involved in after-school activities. It's much easier to allow kids who are afraid to try something new to stay within their comfort zone. But study after study shows that kids who are involved in these types of programs are much less likely to become involved with the wrong kind of friends, alcohol and drugs, violence and gang activity, and premarital sex. Spend the time now encouraging your child to get involved in activities that will enhance their confidence in their own abilities, and you will have much less work to do later. I challenge you to get involved so you can tell whether the coach or Scouting leader is the kind of person you want your child spending time with.

Once again, balance is the key. Some families go to the opposite extreme, overdoing it by allowing—or even urging—their kids to participate in too many sports or activities at the same time.

14. Serving others.

How many times have you heard "The missions trip through our church changed my life forever"? Whenever I talk with youth pastors, I always ask, "What is the single greatest thing you have done to bring the faith of your teens alive?" One very successful youth pastor told me, "I try to get them to live out their faith. Traveling away from their familiar surroundings helps them rely totally on God and his strength to help them fulfill whatever purpose they are there for. Sometimes we build buildings or paint houses or simply go where we can and hand out food to starving people. Serving other people and seeing the destitute lifestyle of those less fortunate is the only surefire way I've found to shake kids out of their complacency."

My own daughter grew tremendously the summer she got involved in a teen-volunteer program. She chose to work at the local retirement home. Being involved with older people—seeing their genuine appreciation and youthful attitudes—was a life-changing experience for her. All she did was serve. Whatever needed to be done, she was asked to do. She volunteered her time, but from her excitement you would have thought she had earned a million dollars.

I receive hundreds of letters from teens each year talking about depression and suicide. Seldom do I encounter a depressed or worried teen who is involved in the lives of those less fortunate. Without realizing it, we automatically count our blessings when we are in situations where we are confronted with people who have very little.

Go with your teen and serve supper at a gospel mission. Have them take clothes they haven't worn in the past six months to Goodwill. Ask your church about the possibility of having several families take a missions trip. There is most likely a place in your own town where you could get involved in the lives of troubled families. Jesus taught us that if we are truly his friends and followers we will look for people to serve. Help your children learn to serve others for the love of the Lord.

15. A close walk and friendship with Jesus.
I put this point last for emphasis, but in reality it needs to be first and foremost—a *foundation* for all the other fourteen assets. There are two main scenarios that can produce in a young person's life a close walk with Jesus as Lord, Savior, and best friend: Either the teen has been fortunate enough to live in a family where most of these fourteen other assets exist, or the young person comes from a very dysfunctional home and has somehow found and clung tightly to Jesus for survival.

It seems very obvious that most of our troubles would be

eliminated if this one point were reality in our lives. But for a young person a close walk with the Lord seldom happens unless he or she is drawn to it by the lifestyle of a hero or loved one.

If any or all of these points seem impossible to you—or too good to be true—please grab hold of the Lord's hand and turn yourself and your problems over to him. He has the strength when we feel weak and frail. He has wisdom that can be ours when we feel like the worst parents in the neighborhood, if we but ask for it. Fall deeply in love with Jesus and your children will witness the greatest role model they could ever have. Together you and your loving heavenly Father can turn your dreams of a healthy family into reality. Start today.

How to Be Ready
to Seize the Moment

WHILE WE can never know exactly what's coming our way, we can anticipate and be prepared for the struggles that can consume and ruin many homes. Being prepared is just good, old-fashioned wisdom. Those of us who take a few moments now can save ourselves a lot of heartaches later.

Here are ten different skills that can help us prepare for Satan's greatest game: ruining families and lives! As we look at these, I encourage you to add notes in the margins about specific strengths and habits that I haven't mentioned that God wants *you* to develop.

1. Stay in shape.
If we are going to be parents who seize tough times for the good of our teens and God's glory, we must be in top shape physically, mentally, spiritually, and socially. Look back over chapter 2 where we discussed the four legs of the chair, and see what areas you have neglected. Be diligent and wise by taking care of yourself and carefully watching over your own relationship with God every single day. Realize that as soon as we lose our health, our friends, and God's strength, we are doomed, and our teens will be fighting for survival all alone. Fight to get and stay in

good physical shape. Our goal is to be strong for our kids now and ourselves later. You are a gift from God. Please take care of yourself.

2. Be a student of your child.

This would be a great time to make a list of your teen's strong points, weaknesses, and natural bents. What are the greatest vulnerablilities in your teen? In what areas do you see foolish choices being made? What needs do you see in your teen? Which friends are influencing your child for the better? Which friends are guiding your teen down the wrong path? Has there ever been a struggle with depression, thoughts of suicide, eating disorders, or the desire to be promiscuous? If the police stopped by your home late this evening, what would you suspect they would discuss with you about your child? Please become a student of your kids. Know their fears and joys. Spend lots of time with them. Become comfortable talking with them about issues vital to their life. Parents have never yet regretted doing their homework on their teens. Give your child someone who truly cares and is willing to prove it.

3. Know yourself.

Have you ever noticed that we get attacked in the same weak areas over and over again? Satan sticks with what works. He knows our weaknesses and strengths. Doesn't it make sense that we should know them as well? His desire is to ruin our home— and if that won't work, he'll gladly settle for wrecking our friendship with our kids.

Do you have close, trusted friends who will tell you the truth about your shortcomings? Are you part of an accountability group? Understand that the only time we are weak is when we try to live in our own strength instead of God's. Great athletes know what areas they need to work on. Do you?

4. Know your worst time of day.

For me, evenings are the time I must be on guard so I don't lose my cool and get angry at the kids when I am tired and at the same time trying to spend special moments with them just before bedtime. Do you know the times of day when you are at your worst and most vulnerable? Take a moment and try to track your high and low times—when you feel the strongest as well as the weakest. Many parents have told me that they never realized until they took inventory what their worst and most unguarded time was. It may be Saturday mornings, dinnertime, bedtime, just before school, after the kids return home from school, Sunday mornings, or when trying to get your kids to do homework or clean their rooms. It's a sign of wisdom to know where Satan has attacked and won more times than not in the past. He knows when you are at your worst. Be ready for him!

5. Put your expectations on the elevator.

The elevator is waiting. When you realize you have inappropriate expectations of your children—meeting your needs, applauding your parenting efforts, being perfect, nurturing you when you are hurting—push the down button. Our kids can't and shouldn't be expected to do for us what God is ready, willing, and waiting to do—meet our needs! He wants us to push the up button when we have emptiness to be filled, hurts to be mended, life to be restored, or tears to be wiped away.

Our family, friends, and even we ourselves can't do what only God can do. Evaluate the positions you put others in, especially your kids, and push the up or down button to put your expectations in their proper place.

6. Listen for their cries.

Did you know that today's young people have an amazing way of letting their parents know their needs? They do it silently. They expect us to read their minds, and they get angry when we can't and don't.

When your fourteen-year-old daughter asks to talk to you alone in her room, don't make a twenty-minute phone call. She may never open up about this particular pain or problem again. If your sixteen-year-old gregarious son is far more quiet than normal for several days and your intuition tells you to go talk to him, do it now and don't let him brush you off.

Hundreds of thousands of America's teens have never been taught these important truths:

- Most problems are temporary and not the end of the world.
- God can handle anything.
- It's OK to ask for help.
- Parents are smarter than they look, and they care for their child more than anyone does, besides God.

Be the one to teach them these things so they don't cry alone or wipe away their own tears anymore.

7. Act on the promptings of the Holy Spirit.

When you talk to God through prayer and read his Word to understand his way of thinking, you have two-thirds of his success formula. Most people never take the little bit of extra time to fulfill the last third of the formula: Be still and listen to God! When he prompts you, be wise and act on it.

When God shouts for us to do something and we flat out refuse, we are like the guy who plugged his lamp in but refused to turn on the switch. Many call it "intuition" or just a strong "gut feeling" to do or say something. Often, it's God trying desperately to get our attention.

8. Make sure they know you love them.

After thousands of one-on-one talks with teens about parent problems, I can assure you that this statement is true: When our kids ask us to spend time with them, whether it be throwing a ball or walking the mall, they are really asking, "Do you love me enough to give up your game/newspaper/ hobby/car/friends/work for me?"

Today's culture, void of values and standards, has left many of our kids wondering if they are loved or even lovable, not knowing whom to ask or where to find out and doing almost anything to gain the answer. They will seldom come right out and ask if we love them—but they will do things daily to secretly see if we do.

9. Never react out of anger.

I can't emphasize enough how damaging it is to say or do things out of anger. Many parents stop yelling, shouting put-downs, or physically grabbing and shaking their kids only after counseling or a legal threat. Any of us are capable of doing and saying things in anger that damage others, especially our kids, that we regret later. Do whatever you have to—count to ten, run the other way, wait until another day, keep your mouth shut, ask for help, call for your spouse, friend, neighbor or pastor, *anything*—but stop before you damage your child with words or actions borne out of anger.

If the damage is already done, ask for forgiveness, regroup, and start over. God is waiting to help and heal.

10. Never say "Don't come back!"

Over the years, many parents have shared with me their greatest regret. I share it with you in hopes that you and I don't repeat it with our kids.

The regret I'm referring to results from exasperated parents repeatedly butting heads with a very strong-willed child. Then in anger they kick the teen out of the home. Many never return.

I'm not talking about "tough love" here—the kind of love needed when our kids have been out of control for so long that if we don't get tough the world and police will. Tough love says, "If you are one minute late, you can't come in for the night. You've broken the rules too many times, and I love you too much to continue protecting and covering up for you." There are times when that kind of approach is necessary. But many parents have taken this extreme position when it was really not called for—out of anger rather than as a carefully considered choice—and they have lived to regret it.

One teen was warned not to date the girls from the wrong side of town. He refused to listen. He was in love. His intense loneliness seemed to be filled only when he was with her. Then came the statement the parents have regretted for over twenty years: "If you see her one more time, don't come back!" Today he and his parents are strangers. Guilt and pain surround almost every holiday and those special times where joyful childhood memories should be remembered. It took that son over ten years to make any kind of contact with his parents at all. Now in his mid-forties, he's learning to be a son, and they are trying to be the parents they failed to be the first time around.

Our home should be a refuge for each of us to hide away from a cold, uncaring world. If it's not, let's change it. But remember never to say words you may live to regret. Just as God would never tell us, please never tell your children to leave and not come back.

"Be dressed for service and well prepared, as though you were waiting for your master to return from the wedding feast. Then you will be ready to open the door and let him in the moment he arrives and knocks. There will be special favor for those who are ready and waiting for his return. I tell you, he himself will seat them, put on an apron, and serve them as they sit and eat! He may come in the middle of the night or just before dawn. But whenever he comes, there will be special favor for his servants who are ready!

"Know this: A homeowner who knew exactly when a burglar was coming would not permit the house to be broken into. You must be ready all the time, for the Son of Man will come when least expected." (Luke 12:35-40)

Jesus challenges us to be like the servants who were to be dressed and ready for service, with their lamps burning, so when their master returned from the wedding feast, they could immediately open the door for him.

Just as Jesus wants us to be ready for his unexpected return, as parents we need to be ready for teachable moments when they arrive. As parents, we need to be on constant watch for the opportunity to reinforce one of our family values. Keep loving your kids and look daily for new ways to praise and serve God, and it will become second nature for you to seize the moment instead of your teen.

Please write to me if you have a story to share or would like to tell me how this book has helped you.

Bill Sanders
c/o Tyndale House Publishers, Inc.
P.O. Box 80
Wheaton, IL 60189-0080

Suggested Reading for Parents and Teens

FOR PARENTS

Making Sense of Adolescence: How to Parent from the Heart
John Crudele and Dick Erickson
(Triumph Books, 1995)

This book covers it all—from how to talk with your teens to understanding their feelings. Includes hundreds of quotes from actual teens, giving their point of view.

Ozzie and Harriet Had a Scriptwriter: Making Tough Choices
with Your Teens in the Real World
David R. Veerman
(Tyndale House, 1996)

In my opinion, Dave Veerman is one of the best-kept secrets in Christian writing today. This book will help any parent start off—and stay—on the right track. Very practical and easy to read.

Getting Out of Your Kids' Faces and into Their Hearts
Valerie Bell
(Zondervan, 1995)

If you want to understand how to parent with feeling and authenticity, this book will really inspire you. Very practical and moving. This book will help any parent become more loving and gentle.

Growing Wise in Family Life
Charles R. Swindoll
(Multnomah, 1988)

This book is vital for parents who are trying to live out their faith in front of their kids.

In His Steps
Charles Sheldon
(various publishers)

This book changed my life like no other. You will be inspired to change the way you respond to situations every day of your life after reading this fast-paced novel. After I read this masterpiece, I bought more than fifty copies and gave them away!

What Your Kids Are Up To and In For
Bill Sanders
(Revell, 1996)

Next to the book you have just read, this is the best book for parents that I've written. I surveyed over 7500 teens from all across America to find out what was really going on with them. Any parent or anyone concerned with affecting the lives of young people should read this book.

Letters to Nicole
Tim Smith
(Tyndale House, 1995)

These actual letters, written by a father to his daughter, will help you talk about important issues with your young teen. The book also includes thirty "What do you think?" discussion starters you can use and ten tips on how to have a guided conversation with your teen.

Wait Quietly: Devotions for a Busy Parent
Dean Merrill
(Tyndale House, 1994)

As the title states, this is a great book for busy parents who want to carve out time to spend with the Lord each day. Each reading contains a Scripture passage, some thoughts from Dean Merrill (father of three), and suggestions for putting what you've read to work in your life. The book also contains valuable resources in its appendix: special Scriptures for single mothers, special Scriptures for single fathers, 150 best Scriptures for your child to memorize, and pages to record your family's spiritual highlights.

Why Did You Do That?
Wm. Lee Carter
(Tyndale House, 1996)

This book by a licensed psychologist and family therapist helps you understand why your family members act the way they do. You can learn to "read" behavior as a message board that is telling the world how people feel about themselves. This is especially important when you're trying to love and nurture your teen.

FOR TEENS

How to Live with Your Parents Without Losing Your Mind
Ken Davis
(Zondervan, 1988)

Your kids will love this book and at the same time develop a desire for a closer walk with God without even realizing it. Ken's wit and wisdom really shine through in this award-winning book.

Prisoner of the American Dream
Joseph Jennings
(self-published; to order, call 1-407-723-9528)

Joseph Jennings, an ex–gang member, is a very close friend of mine. His words will change your teen's life forever. In this book he exposes the dangers of drugs, alcohol, and the wrong friends. The first year after he met Jesus and left the gang, he led over ten thousand teens to Christ. Read the inspiring story of one of the top youth speakers in the world today.

Straight Talk for Girls and *Straight Talk for Guys*
Bill Sanders
(Revell, 1996)

Each of these books contains fifty short devotionals. Each devotional is designed to catch a teen's attention with an interesting or gripping story and show that in every situation we find ourselves in, God is there and we have vital choices to make. I'm getting lots of letters telling me that these are being read daily, challenging young people to live like Jesus.

Life, Sex, and Everything in Between: Straight-on Answers to the Questions That Trouble You Most
Bill Sanders
(Revell, 1991)

I receive over two thousand letters from teens each school year, and this book contains my answers to the top seventy-five questions they ask. Young adults will find multiple-step answers to help them deal with problems that seem insurmountable to them.

Teen Power: Treasury of Solid Gold Advice for Teens by Several Top Youth Communicators
(Chess Press Publishers; to order, call 1-800-899-9543 or 612-942-6207)

This is a *Chicken Soup for the Soul* type of book especially for teens. The character and compassion of each of these speakers makes this a life-changing book. I believe thousands of lives will be changed forever as a result of reading this timely, inspirational book.

Making a Love That Lasts—Without Having to Settle for Sex
Jacob Aranza
(Servant Publishers, 1996)

Most teens are looking for acceptance, approval, and affection and are trying to meet those needs with sex. Jacob Aranza, a masterful storyteller, knows teens. He helps them find lasting relationships instead of settling for second best. Jacob will help your teen be on God's path and look for God's best when it comes to long-term relationships. A must read!

When Your Parents Pull Apart
Angela Elwell Hunt
(Tyndale House, 1995)

Through the journal entries of a fictional teenage girl mixed with great, practical advice from Angie Hunt, teens learn how to deal with some of the heartbreaking issues that hit them when their parents get divorced. If your teens are facing this situation, this book can help.